DEATH: A PREFACE

(A Continuing Journey)

by HAL N. BANKS, S.T.D.

toExcel
San Jose New York Lincoln Shanghai

Death: A Preface
(A Continuing Journey)

All Rights Reserved © 1987, 2000 by Hal N. Banks

No part of this book may be reproduced or transmitted in any form or by any means, graphic, electronic, or mechanical, including photocopying, recording, taping, or by any information storage or retrieval system, without the permission in writing from the publisher.

Published by toExcel
an imprint of iUniverse.com, Inc.

For information address:
iUniverse.com, Inc.
620 North 48th Street
Suite 201
Lincoln, NE 68504-3467
www.iuniverse.com

ISBN: 0-595-00212-9

Printed in the United States of America

Dedication

To my wife, Phyllis Eileen,
longsuffering; my editor, critic
and confidant.

"*She speaks with wisdom, and
faithful instruction is on her tongue.*"
Proverbs 31:26

And to our children:

Linda, Ken, Randy, Jean, Susan and Scott

My special thanks to the following for editorial assistance: Scott Banks, Helen and John Bierstein, Kay and Ray Lewis, and Cynthia Roe Smith.

Also by Hal N. Banks:

Introduction to Psychic Studies

CONTENTS

Preface i
   I. The Tyranny of Fear. 1
  II. Survival Defined 12
 III. The Indications of Survival 18
 IV. Our Adventure Following Death. 55
  V. The Moments of Transition. 63
 VI. First Steps 69
VII. The Whole of the Matter 83
VIII. Growth in the Ways of Spirit. 90
 IX. Everyday Life on the Other Side 99
  X. Preparation for Our Journey in Spirit 106
 XI. Shalom 119
  II. Questions I've Been Asked 129
Schema for What Happens After Death. 137
Bibliography 139

"The question for man most momentous of all is whether or no he has an immortal soul, or ...whether or no his personality involves any element which can survive bodily death."
   F. W. H. Myers

PREFACE

What happens when we die? This question strikes at the very roots of our being; no other equals it in importance. It kindles every emotion, gives perspective to life and underscores the urgency of coming to terms with our eternal destiny. Sigmund Freud believed that death is "The oldest, strongest and most insistent wish of mankind."[1]

If we are honest and open minded in our thinking, we no longer need to be mired in a morass of doubt when we ask what awaits us when we cross the threshold between this world and the next.

To help you form a new and positive philosophy about life after death, I would like to place before you, for your consideration, an unfoldment of your continuing evolution beyond the point of physical death. This will be based on a flood of information from some of the most respected and disciplined minds in the field of religion and psychical research. The recorded evidence is too voluminous, consistent and dependable to dispute or certainly ignore. It is, to say the least, strongly suggestive of proof, and founded upon records and illustrations that reflect the spontaneous and anecdotal in psychical research.

John J. Heaney in his book, *The Sacred & the Psychic*, tells us "If we reach conclusions which are only highly probable, strongly probable or almost overwhelmingly probable, one cannot wash one's hands of the subject while saying, 'But it has not been scientifically proven...'"[2]

It is foolish to accept the axiom that science is the only infallible avenue to truth. It is also unfortunate that tradition and rigidity of mind have ossified our ability to decide critical issues for ourselves; especially when such issues involve our final destiny.

The descriptive chapters of this book, a schematic of what happens when we discard our physical clothing, will give emphasis to a number of vital and relevant concerns. They are:

1. that we need and can cultivate a completely realistic, reasonable and logical philosophy of life, a theology, centered on what actually happens when we step out of our physical bodies;

2. that death is not the cessation of life, but a change of form or condition;

3. that life after death for all persons is a part of God's natural order, and that it is impossible to be separated from Him;

4. that we need not fear death, but should consider it a welcome friend;

5. that our final destiny, as it is so often depicted in traditional theology, is not at all congruent with reality;

6. that heaven and hell are subjective states of mind and not geographical locations;

7. that we do not live by faith alone;

8. that God has a specific plan for each life and that ultimately, beyond the space-time continuum we are familiar with, that plan will come to complete and total fruition.

It is imperative that we escape some of the suffocating dogma and traditional theology that have held us in bondage for centuries. Hopefully, this book might provide some of the keys to your liberation.

Must reading for clear insights into the devastating effect fundamentalism has on adherents is an eye opening book, *Holy Terror*, by Flo Conway and Jim Siegelman. The open warfare being waged on our freedom is clearly delineated and is frightening in its scope. The authors peg it as a declared holy war for the soul of America.

My book, then, is a volume about life, your life, when you step out of your physical frame to experience that epochal adventure; another step toward the realization of all that you are intended to be. For now we see but shadows, a semblance of existence, but death will reveal substance and a far greater authenticity.

Joy comes in knowing that at the culmination of our earthly pilgrimage, our personality, complete with memory and character will survive.

My wish is that this book will provide you with a fresh approach to a marvelous adventure that awaits each of us when we cross the threshold of death.

Death *is* a preface, a continuing journey.

> *"This life of mortal breath*
> *Is but a suburb of the life*
>   *elysian,*
> *Whose portal we call death."*
>   – Longfellow's *Resignation*

Sources of Information:

My involvement in psychical research began in 1965. In that year I was determined to begin a systematic study of the best and most reliable literature available; literature of stature and integrity. My first steps in exploration and research included such classics as F. W. H. Myers' *Human Personality and Its Survival of Bodily Death*; *On the Edge of the Etheric* by Arthur Findlay and *Man's Survival After Death*, by Charles Tweedale.

I was both heartened and amazed at the number of titles, past and present, that were attainable. How they escaped my attention during my seminary training and early years of ministry will always remain a mystery. I carefully avoided the purely sensational and frothy escapist books, and confined my reading and research to the foundational literature written by individuals of great probity, insight and wisdom; in short, the heavyweights of psychical research.

Thus, in preparation for this book, I have consulted the following:

(1) *The Proceedings and Journals of the British Society for Psychical Research* from 1882 to the present, as well as similar documents published by the American Society for Psychical Research.
(2) The definitive literature, past and present, that speaks directly to the subject under discussion, survival of consciousness. This consisted of hundreds of books that throw ample light on the topic, such as the writings of Emanuel Swedenborg, especially *Heaven and Hell*; Anthony Borgia's trilogy; Robert Crookall's writings, especially *The Supreme Adventure*; Paul Beard's *Survival of Death*; Stainton Moses' *Spirit Teachings*; Charles Drayton Thomas' *Life Beyond Death with Evidence*; the writings of Geraldine Cummins, especially *The Road to Immortality*; Arthur Findlay's *On the Edge of the Etheric*; Broads' *Lectures on Psychical Research*; *Psychic Exploration*, edited by John White; *The Great Books of the Western World*; the four volumes of the *Encyclopedia of Philosophy*; *God, Man and Thinker* by Donald A. Wells; and Elton Trueblood's Philosophy of Religion; The volumes listed above represent just a few that I consulted. My bibliography indicates the scope of my reading and research.
(3) Numerous publications were consulted, such as *Theta*; *The Journal of Religion and Psychical Research*; *The Christian Parapsychologist*; Parapsychology Review; and the Quarterly *Journal of Spiritual Frontiers Fellowship*.
(4) The records of the various sittings I have had with gifted sensitives such as George Daisley of Santa Barbara, California, Ena Twigg and Douglas Johnson of the United Kingdom.
(5) The many individuals I have interviewed and who have given generously of their time.
(6) The Scriptures of the world's living religions.
(7) A vast number of theological sources, liberal and conservative. In addition to the books this includes such magazines as *The Christian Century* and *Christianity Today*. Numerous pamphlets were also noted and read.
(8) The hundreds of students I have had in my classes over the

years.

My research has been as thorough as possible, but I want to emphasize the above mentioned materials are generally available for your own personal study and enjoyment. It is vital that you do your own research and not depend on my personal observations and comments. Follow the advice of the Scriptures: "Why don't you judge for yourselves what is right." (Luke 12:57).

This book, then, is a distillation of my research, study and beliefs.

       Hal N. Banks
       Roswell, New Mexico 1987

SOURCE NOTES

1. *Time* Magazine. November 12, 1965. Vol. 86, Number 20, p.53.
2. Heaney, John J. *The Sacred and the Psychic.* New York: Paulist Press, 1984, p.16.

The source of all Scriptural quotations used in this book is the New International Version unless otherwise indicated. Published by the Zondervan Corporation for the New York International Bible Society, 1978.

Note: I use the pronoun *he* throughout the book and trust my readers will understand it is used strictly in a generic sense and does not imply male chauvinism.

*"Death is not the enemy;
living in constant fear
of it is..."*
— Norman Cousins

CHAPTER 1

The Tyranny of Fear

"If I had only one sermon to preach it would be a sermon against fear." The speaker was not a preacher but G. K. Chesterton, the noted English writer. This was his answer when a British publishing company, planning to publish a volume of sermons, asked him if he could only preach one sermon, what would be his subject.

His choice was highly significant because fear is very high on the list when you catalog the number of books on this subject in the nation's book stores. Thomas Hobbs, English political philosopher, put this into perspective when he said, "Myself and fear were born twins." While many fears tyrannize us and are enemies of a healthy body, mind and soul, not all fears are damaging. Normal fear is indispensable and wholly acceptable. Fear prevents us from walking over the edge of a precipice or into the path of a car. Norman Vincent Peale says, and wisely, that "Without normal fear a person cannot be a well organized personality."[1]

Death the Ultimate Fear

I am convinced that the word death with its multitudinous mental connections can produce intimidating fear.

The word death, especially with its theological coloring, can trigger an enervating fear that is devastating to the personality. The word speaks of a certain finality, termination and extinction. It cancels the personalilty's long struggle to attain some degree of spiritual and mental maturity. To hear the word death, which is so solidly engrained in our vocabulary, brings to mind a host of upsetting mental images such as the grim reaper, deceased, grave, casket, funeral, hell and the last judgment.

Now quickly substitute the word life for death. What are your mental images now? Pleasant? Life is the opposite of death. We immediately think of growth, aliveness, alertness, vigor, spirit, briskness, energy and activity. When I use the term death, I use it only in reference to the door that the incident opens. Beyond that door is life; life abundant. Death is a preface, a prelude to expansion of consciousness.

Ernest Becker, author of *The Denial of Death*, has said that at the bottom of all of our phobias lies the fear of death. The dread of dying is called thanatophobia. Several years ago there was a woman in one of my classes who was terribly frightened of death. It was an overriding fear and so devastating that it fragmented her day to day living. Following one of my sessions on the survival of personality, she came up to me and said, "Hal, my fear is gone and I'm free at last. Thank you." Let me assure you that death is a friend and not the enemy, so let not your hearts be troubled.

In John Mundy's book, *Learning to Die*, he tells us that "Research has revealed that actually most dying people do face death unafraid, and may even die happily."[2]

Dr. Karlis Osis, in interviews with dying patients, revealed "...that considerable numbers of patients meet death not with fear and despair but rather with elation and exaltation. (Osis cites the remarks of a hospital resident) ...Great anxiety building up for days, that usually disappears 1-3 hours before death...A general practitioner remarked that...There is such a resigned, peaceful, almost happy expression which comes over the patient - it is hard to explain but it leaves me with the feeling that I would not be afraid to die..."[3]

A medical doctor, William Hunter, was near death when he said, "If I had strength enough to hold a pen, I would write how easy and pleasant a thing it is to die."

Many associated with the medical profession who have witnessed the death of patients have remarked how they have made the transition very peacefully and gratefully. There is absolutely nothing to fear, for love is far stronger than death.

Fundamentalism – Its Legacy of Fear

I am now opening a Pandora's box by talking about fear that is directly attributable to the preaching and teaching of the fundamentalist wing of the Christian Church. The fear engendered is as poisonous to our well-being as any with which I am familiar. It leaves a terrible legacy and scars personalities, in many instances beyond psychological repair. Theological teaching and preaching in the fundamentalist camp have often used fear as a weapon.

Fundamentalism takes its cue from the Bible. The heart of fundamentalism is that the Scriptures are considered to be infallible and without error. Adherents are slavishly and unalterably bound to the written Word. It is a form of idolatry; worship of the Word itself. In his book, *Rediscovering the Bible*, Bernhard W. Anderson tells us, "...Fundamentalism is really a form of bibliolatry, that is, it is a faith in the Bible itself, rather than faith in the God who speaks his Word through the Bible..."[4] Inerrancy of the Scriptures is the first line of defense in the fundamentalist theological and ecclesiastical structure.

Coincident with this intolerant bibliolatry is the setting forth of certain fundamentals such as: (1) the infallibility, inspiration and inerrancy of the Scriptures; they are to be understood literally; (2) the virgin birth and deity of Christ; (3) the substitutionary theory of the atonement. Christ died for our sins; (4) the doctrine of the Trinity; and (5) the bodily resurrection, ascension and second coming of Christ. To deny any one of these so-called fundamentals demolishes the total house of cards. The dissenter becomes x-rated, a spiritual drop-out and earmarked for eternal damnation.

Edward John Carnell, writing in *A Handbook for Christian Theology* explains, "Fundamentalism is a paradoxical position. It sees the heresy in untruth but not in unloveliness. If it has the most truth, it has the least grace, since it distrusts courtesy and diplomacy. Fundamentalism forgets that orthodox truth without orthodox love profits nothing. The more it departs from the gentle ways of Jesus Christ, the more it drives urbane people from the fold of orthodoxy..."[5]

Fundamentalism can be militant and repressive. It teaches people how to hate. It can be devastatingly disruptive and divisive.

Why then is fundamentalism so attractive to so many people? In times of great social unrest and emotional stress, some measure of stability is sought. We live in a world tormented by extreme violence. Drugs and sexual promiscuity are rampant. Ethical dishonesty in government is almost commonplace. Fundamentalism seemingly places a solid foundation underneath the vast instability of the world in which we live.

Dogmatic fundamentalism can be a virulent form of totalitarianism in masquerade. A religion of creeds, dogma and authority becomes a burden and leads to inflexibility and rigid intolerance. The price we pay is incalculable. Authoritarian religion, predicated upon sacrosanct articles of belief, will not allow for the slightest deviation. To dare to put one's foot into the middle of the Fundamentalist Christian's cauldron of inviolable theological beliefs brings immediate vehement censure and denunciation as a tool of the devil. Fundamentalism's legacy is fear.

We Must Be Free to Choose

Blind faith in anything is highly dangerous. Authoritarianism is its disciple. Only as we are presented with alternatives are we free to choose. Our personal philosophy of life must ultimately be the product of our own quest for truth as we sort through a multitude of options that almost daily bombard us. But it is only as we are faithful to our inner feelings, that inner authority, that we attain our true spiritual stature.

Emanuel Swedenborg, famed natural scientist and theologian, explains that, "Faith is an internal acknowledgment of truth."

Only when that innate core of sensitivity is touched do you become an authentic person; only as you personally respond to something within can truth be life-changing. It is too bad that so many people are more interested in authoritarian claims than in truth itself.

So, approach what I say with caution, always keeping the above thoughts in mind. My understanding of reality is partial and intensely subjective. It accords with my personal world view. No one individual has all the answers. Consult those who argue differently and then accept what rings true for you.

Discard the rest, and place it in the upper levels of your mind for further reference.

An Escape from Fear

What alternatives do we have? Perhaps my personal spiritual manifesto will be suggestive as you struggle to build a contemporary theological framework.

(1) Religion is a very private matter. Do not accept anything anyone tells you you must believe, because truth for you must meet your own inward spiritual needs.

(2) Each of us is different with unique spiritual needs. A homogenized religion assaults and does violence to our individuality. Just as God has a different plan for each person, so must that design include spiritual resources relevant to that individual's particular needs. This is just common sense and in accord with logic.

(3) The right to dissent from established or traditional dogma or beliefs is crucial to our personal search for religious truth.

(4) No belief or creed must be considered inviolate. Change is our only constant. Our belief systems must undergo constant scrutiny. What today is applicable to our spiritual pilgrimage may be irrelevant tomorrow.

The Open and Closed Mind

The closed minded do not carefully analyze, criticize and scrutinize alternative beliefs. Anything that is alien to what they personally espouse is relegated to the wastebasket. Such individuals isolate themselves from anything that strays from what they have been told to believe.

If you closely examine the beliefs of narrow and intolerant persons you frequently discover that they tend to contradict themselves. They fail to note their mutually exclusive statements primarily because they are mouthing the beliefs of someone else, frequently theological declarations heard from a pulpit. They neglect to examine or question what they have heard. The information is second-hand. Such individuals are not their own authorities, but are other-directed.

A fundamentalist minister once questioned my right to be a clergyman because of my interest in psychical research. He wanted my denomination to defrock me. I told him I would like to talk with him about psychic phenomena and recommended five books I felt he should read to be reasonably well informed. He refused, for this would give the "devil" an opportunity to corrupt his life. This fundamentalist clergyman knew absolutely nothing about psychical research except what he had been told by informants antagonistic to the subject. However, he did cuddle at the foot of the fundamentals of traditional theology. This is an example of a closed mind.

Conversely, the open-minded person is one who is always willing to listen to divergent beliefs and to evaluate what he believes. He is not offended when alternative beliefs are presented and discussed and, if the occasion warrants, he readily makes changes in his personal belief system.

We do not live in a static universe and only the fool clings to outworn and irrelevant convictions. The quest for truth is ongoing. Nothing can ultimately defame the truth, and the only way to discover it is to keep our minds open and flexible.

Evaluate. Question. Assess. Judge. Do not permit any person to make up your mind for you. You are your own authority in spiritual matters. It is within, and not without, that truth is discovered. Gamaliel had very germane and incisive words for the authoritarian when He said, "But if it is from God, you will not be able to stop these men; you will only find yourselves fighting against God." (Acts 5:39)

The Fear of Hell

While a repressive fundamentalism does provide spiritual sustenance for some, it does have a deleterious effect on personality. Psychological aberrations, such as fear and guilt, frequently result from allegiance to such a rigid and inflexible theological portfolio. This is strikingly evident in the dogma surrounding the death experience. Those who have been fed a steady diet of the once and for all choice of either heaven or hell are frequently mentally harassed throughout their lives as to whether they will be eligible for the greener pastures of heaven or the abode of eternal fire and brimstone.

A number of years ago someone gave me a small religious tract written by a Jimmy Allen, Dallas, Texas. Without qualification he speaks of hell as eternal. "The punishment will continue forever and ever and ever.... There won't be any God to listen to you scream and beg for mercy...hell is a place of fire...a place of pain; a place where the wicked are tormented; there'll be no relief for you...After man has been in hell a hundred, thousand, million, billion, trillion years, he has no less time to stay...Hell is a hopeless and helpless place."[6]

This tract is venomous, fear saturated and a horribly distorted portrayal, not of God, but of a fiend. The fear and guilt produced by such an abhorrent theology, if you dare call it a theology, is beyond measure. Death in such writings is to be feared, and the thought of not knowing which gate you will ultimately enter creates a life of frustration and uncertainty.

An ordained minister, a product of a home where fundamentalism was taught and practiced, told me that he could not shake the vestiges of his past despite the fact he wanted to graduate beyond such theological opinions. He was tormented by the grip his earlier teachings had upon him. He felt guilty that he had departed from the path his parents had prescribed. What a tragedy.

Wouldn't it be a blessing to grow from childhood, through adulthood, to old age not having endured any of this constant barrage about God's wrath, judgment and hell?

In M. H. Tester's *The Bewildered Man's Guide to Death* he says "The first thing you must do is to put aside all the childish teachings that have been cluttering your mind for so long. Try and drain your mind of everything you have been taught about death. Forget heaven and hell, cleanse your thoughts of the alternatives of the boredom of being waited on hand and foot by platonic houris while you idly twang your harp, or of being tormented and toasted and tortured by devils."[7] We can be taught to fear death. There is a conditioning. We respond in infancy, especially, to the conduct, control and thinking of our parents. Our emotional lives can be dominated by the images of fear instilled in us, especially by theologically authoritarian parents.

But if, as the vast findings of psychical research indicate, there is no death, we can then build upon the twin foundations of hope and certainty. What, then is there to fear? Each of us has eternity to fully realize God's incredibly marvelous plan for our lives. We can thus live our lives confident of the resplendent promise of our Creator; that He is God of the living and not of the dead.

Another realistic way to cope with fear is to disarm it with humor. The following true illustrations were given to me by my wife's sister, Carol.

"For years, if someone wanted to borrow money from this man, he always smiled and said, 'Sorry, all I have is a couple of dollars I'll need to get home on.'"

"The other thing we remember about him was his love for White Castle coffee. He said he would know he was in heaven when he died if there was a White Castle restaurant there.

"When he died, his wife walked up to his casket. She looked in the breast pocket on his suit and patted it. 'Yes, there you are, Honey,' she said 'your White Castle coupons and a couple of dollars in case you get a chance to come home.'"

The other illustration tells of a 96-year-old woman who was vivacious, full of life and loved to play poker, especially if a little money was involved.

When she died her son put four aces and a wild card up the sleeve of her dress. He said, "There you are, Mom, you're going out with a winning hand."

His sister-in-law, standing nearby, heard him and as she slipped a couple of dollars in the other sleeve, she said, "That's fine, but you didn't give her anything to bet with. Now she is all set."

The above illustrations show how some people can accept death as only a transition, and that life does continue in another dimension. This book is meant to be an antidote to fear. As I bring this chapter to a close, I want to share with you a happy experience of Ruth Eimer, a friend living here in Roswell, New Mexico.

"When I was 18 years old, I was in nurses training at Bellevue Hospital School of Nursing, New York City. At that time the prevailing medical opinion was that tonsils were catchers of disease germs. Accordingly, all student nurses who still had tonsils were expected to have them removed. They scheduled one day for tonsillectomies for student nurses. On that day there were 5 or 6 of us waiting to have the operation. One by one we were removed to the operating room. Finally there were only two of us left, and, of course, we were nervous. My friend asked to be next and she was scared. After they started to operate on her, they gave me anesthesia. For some reason they ran into difficulties with her and I was under longer than the normal time.

"While I was still anesthesized, I became very frightened. I thought I was in a long dark tunnel and moving quite rapidly. I grew more and more frightened. Suddenly everything grew brighter and I saw a tall figure clothed in a radiant long white robe. I thought it must be Jesus.

"He reached out and took my hand and immediately I was at peace and filled with joy. The area about me was light and beautiful. We communicated but without speaking. It was by thought.

"I have two sisters. Esther is much like the Biblical Martha while Mary is like the Bible's Mary. The being of light told me Esther was like a needle – straight and fun. Mary was like a fluffy ball of cotton. This sounded very strange to me, but it was very clear. It was an explanation of what they were like.

"Even further, I learned the secret of life – it was so simple! I thought 'If only everyone knew it how happy we'd all be.'

"I was enjoying myself so much when he suddenly said, 'It's time for you to go back now.' I kept protesting, but to no avail.

"Then suddenly I awakened in my hospital bed with my friends around me.

"I firmly believe I had died, and since that time I have had no fear of dying. I know how beautiful it is when we make the transition. I can no longer remember what I was told about the secret of life, but, if I were to hazard a guess, it would be love."

IN SUMMARY

1. The poison of fear is widespread in our society.
2. Normal fear is indispensable and acceptable.
3. The fear of death is the ultimate fear.
4. When we substitute the word life in place of death our fear of death is lessened.
5. Some research indicates that most individuals at the point of death welcome it and have little fear.

6. The fundamentalist wing of the Christian faith leaves a terrible legacy of fear as a result of its preaching and teaching.
7. The root of the fundamentalist problem is its insistence that the Bible be interpreted literally.
8. A rigid fundamentalism attracts adherents because of the instability of our times.
9. A religion of creeds, dogma and authority can be burdensome and be the direct cause of fear and other psychological problems.
10. Blind faith in anything is dangerous. We must consider alternatives and be free to choose what it is we believe. Our beliefs must be right for us and must satisfy our personal quest for truth.
11. A person with a closed and inflexible mind can be intolerant of any who might disagree with him.
12. A person with an open and flexible mind constantly evaluates what he believes and isn't afraid to discard untenable and outworn beliefs.
13. Always remember you are your own authority, especially in spiritual matters.
14. Death is the ultimate fear because of what we have been taught about hell.
15. The fear of the Biblical hell has caused untold psychological damage in our society.
16. The findings of psychical research and an intelligent interpretation of the Bible should fill us with hope and great certainty.
17. I would urge you to erase from your mind any fear of death. Begin with the premise that THERE IS NO DEATH.

SOURCE NOTES

(1) Peale, Norman Vincent. *Guide to Confident Living.* New York: Prentice-Hall, 1948, p. 130.
(2) Mundy, Jon. *Learning to Die.* Evanston, Illinois: Spiritual Frontiers Fellowship, 1973, p.14.
(3) Osis, Karlis. *Deathbed Observations by Physicians and Nurses.*

New York: Parapsychology Foundation, Inc., 1961, p.23.
(4) Anderson, Bernhard W. *Rediscovering the Bible.* New York: Association Press, 1951, p.17.
(5) Carnell, Edward John. *Fundamentalism.* In *A Handbook of Christian Theology*, Marvin Halverson (ed.), New York: World Publishing, 1958, p. 142.
(6) Allen, Jimmy. *What is Hell Like?* Dallas, Texas, Christian Tracts, (No Publication Date Given). (Pamphlet).
(7) Tester, M. H. *The Bewildered Man's Guide to Death.* London: The Psychic Press, 1964, p. 7. (Pamphlet).

"We have reached a point where further proof is superfluous, and where the weight of disproof lies upon those who deny."
— Sir Arthur Conan Doyle

CHAPTER II

Survival Defined

Definition of the Word Survival

Before examining the major categories giving evidence supporting survival, the word itself must be defined.

Survival would acknowledge a post-mortem embodied existence whereby the individual would be a thinking, feeling and willing self-conscious person. Simply put, survival for you will mean a continuance of your personality in another state of consciousness following the death of your physical body. You will interact with others and will be fully aware of your surroundings.

It would follow, then, that our spiritual or etheric body is solid and a duplicate of our former physical body but without its imperfections. We will be identifiable; substantial. In other words it has form, wholeness. It is perfect, totally free of blemish and earthly limitation. Those on earth who suffered the loss of a limb, or had a crippling disease, were blind or deaf, are now completely free of such disabilities.

The Severe Limitations of Our Sense Organs

In consideration of what I have just said, it should be mentioned how severely limited our sense organs are. It is impossible to avoid sensory contact in our daily round of activity, and this can blind us to the greater reality that is non-sensory. We are bound to our physical and material existence to the extent that we are unaware of what lies beyond what we can see, smell, taste, touch or hear. The unseen world is the eternal, permanent world. What we now enjoy is fleeting and transitory. The writer of II Corinthians 4:18 spells it out quite simply: "...So we fix our eyes not on what is seen, but on what is unseen." The ancients grasped this point more significantly than we sophisticated moderns.

In his fascinating book, *The Unobstructed Universe*, Stewart Edward White gives an illustration that lends immediacy and meaning to what I am saying. The book is an account of communication he had with his wife on the other side of physical death. She emphatically makes the point that we live in one universe and not two. In the contact she had with her husband, she cites his inability to perceive more than his personal circumscribed world. His wife tells him: "...What I am really trying to say is that I live in the universe you don't see, and also in the one you do see. Therefore, I live in the *whole* universe."[1]

This illustration indicates the great limitations of our sensory organs and how incomprehensibly vast the world is beyond our sense perceptions. Thus any consideration of survival evidence must inevitably keep the insufficiency of our sensory make-up clearly in mind. Carl G. Jung reminds us that, "...We are strictly limited by our innate structure and therefore bound by our whole being and thinking to this world..."[2]

Science is Not the Sole Avenue to Truth

We are hung up on the role science plays in our lives. It is only if something can be verified, replicated, weighed or measured by the strict canons of science, that we accept it as fact. What may look to be impossible, removed from the canons of common sense, illogical, contradictory and completely contrary to what we have come to expect and know, does not mean that it isn't true. Non-verifiable psychic phenomena, rich in illusive and suggestive patterns, yield what for many is convincing evidence for life after death. Such consistent and cumulative information, contributed over many years by thoroughly competent and reliable individuals, cannot be explained away.

Professor William James, an illuminating personality, with credentials in medicine, philosophy and psychology, graphically registers my complete sentiments when he said: "...If you wish to upset the law that all crows are black, you must not seek to show that no crows are; it is enough if you prove one single crow to be white..."[3]

In *The Lives of a Cell* by essayist and medical doctor Lewis Thomas a line corroborates what I've been saying: "...Something can be highly improbable, maybe almost impossible, and at the same time true."[4]

The Spontaneous-Anecdotal Approach

The path I have followed in this book concerns spontaneous-anecdotal information relating to survival of human personality. It does not have the academic coloring associated with its close ally, parapsychology. Such information relates primarily to those who have had psychic experiences that are unplanned and unanticipated. They usually occur spontaneously as men and women are about their everyday routines.

For instance, my wife and I have on two different occasions been almost overpowered by the smell of grape-fragrance. We couldn't find any reasonable or logical explanation for what happened. Both occasions were completely unexpected and caught us by surprise.

These two exciting psychic experiences reflect on what must be the strong desire of friends and relatives who have predeceased us to literally say, "Hey, look, we're alive and we want you to know this. "Why the grape fragrance? Those of us close to the ministry would relate to the grape in that the juice is used in our communion services, so what better way for discarnates to get our attention?

A student of mine in Alaska, relates her personal experience: "In 1970 my father died a very unexpected and quick death. There was no way that I could prepare myself for it. I had been extremely close to him, much closer than any of my brothers and sister and I was in a bad state of shock when it happened. When I went to bed that night, I was afraid that I would be unable to sleep but I drifted into slumber very quickly. I saw my father floating/flying with his arms and hands by his sides over the greenest, flattest countryside I had ever seen. The light was extraordinarily bright and the smile on his face was absolutely beautiful. He looked so young and so happy. That dream helped me through the next several weeks and months, and in fact still helps me."

John J. Heaney, writing in his book, *The Sacred and the Psychic*, makes a strong point in these words: "Science is interested in strict proof according to its own paradigms. But human beings are interested in the real, whether reached by strict science or by some other means."[5]

Spontaneous-anecdotal experiences abound. Witness Paul's vision found in II Corinthians 12:2-4. He relates: "...I know a man in Christ who fourteen years ago was caught up to the third heaven. Whether it was in the body or out of the body-God knows. And I know that this man...was caught up to Paradise. He heard inexpressible things, things that man is not permitted to tell..."

To note the wealth of spontaneous-anecdotal material available for study and research, one need only read a few pages of F. W. H. Myers' seminal work, *Human Personality and Its Survival of Bodily Death*, and *Phantasms of the Living* by three of the founders of the Society for Psychical Research, F. W. H. Myers, Edmund Gurney and Frank Podmore.

A particularly gripping spontaneous experience appears in Myers' work. The illustration originally appeared in the eighth volume of the Proceedings of the Society for Psychical Research, and concerns a minister's wife, Mrs. E. K. Elliott:

"About 20 years ago I received some letters by post, one of which contained fifteen pounds in bank notes. After reading the letters I went into the kitchen with them in my hands. I was alone at the time...Having done with the letters, I made a motion to throw them into the fire, when I distinctly felt my hand arrested in the act. It was as though another hand were gently laid upon my own, pressing it back. Much surprised, I looked at my hand, and then saw that it contained not the letters I had intended to destroy, but the bank notes, and that the letters were in the other hand. I was so surprised that I called out, 'Who is here?' I called the cook and told her, and also told my husband on the first opportunity. I never had any similar experience before or since."

Her husband, the Rev. E. K. Elliott, corroborates her story.

Parapsychology: The Scientific Approach

J. B. Rhine, sometimes referred to as the "Father of Parapsychology," coined that formidable term. Beginning in the early 1930's the science of parapsychology was established and the vast investigative effort was launched. Experimental procedures, using the tools of the laboratory, dominated the work of the infant discipline. The quantitative search had begun in earnest and continues. For the purist, the word parapsychology should only describe paranormal activity placed under the scrutiny of the laboratory with its preciseness and exactness.

Most psychic research activity is today predominately centered in the canons of science where all research is done within the framework of the scientific method. Replication, or repeatability of experiments, is the heart of the matter. However, there has been a noticeable shift of interest back to the spontaneous-anecdotal approach to psychic matters, with all its credible information. Both paths are completely valid.

John Beloff, parapsychologist at the University of Edinburgh, puts the matter quite convincingly when he candidly states, "Don't be bullied into believing that anecdotal evidence can't be admitted into the body of science...We can't dispense with human testimony in dealing with human events. Lawyers and historians have developed their own criteria for assessing the quality of the testimony on which they have to rely. Parapsychologists have similarly developed their own criteria. The strongest reason for believing in the reality of psi is personal experience."[6]

IN SUMMARY

1. A definition of survival would be to say that the personality of each individual continues in an identifiable substantial form following physical death.
2. This post-mortem body is free of all blemishes and disabilities.
3. Our sensory organs are severely limited.

4. The unseen world is the permanent, real and enduring world.
5. The universe is unobstructed and one.
6. Science is not the sole avenue to the discovery of truth.
7. Things that appear illogical and contradictory may at times be productive of truth.
8. The spontaneous-anecdotal approach, employed in this book, concerns everyday, unplanned and completely spontaneous psychic happenings of ordinary people.
9. Parapsychology is the scientific study of psychic phenomena.

SOURCE NOTES

(1) White, Stewart Edward. *The Unobstructed Universe.* New York: E. P. Dutton and Company, Inc., p. 59.
(2) Jung, Carl G. *Memories, Dreams, Reflections.* New York: Vintage Books, 1961, p.300.
(3) James, William. *Human Immortality.* New York: Dover Publications, Inc., 1956, p.319.
(4) Thomas, Lewis. *The Lives of a Cell.* New York: Viking Press, 1974, p.140.
(5) Heaney, John J. *The Sacred & the Psychic.* New York: Paulist Press, 1984, p. 78.
(6) Beloff, John. *Fate Magazine* , November, 1983, p. 14.

"In my opinion information about our future life, with its practical implications, is the goal to which all psychic phenomena and evidence should lead."
    – Charles Drayton Thomas

Chapter III

The Indications of Survival

In consideration of matters concerning survival of consciousness, the question that we must ask ourselves is, "What would convince me that survival is fact?"

I am submitting for your study and consideration 27 areas that speak clearly to the matter of survival of consciousness. These areas are cited as evidential.

1. Indications of evidence based on the consistency of reports concerning the same experiences.

2. Indications of evidence based on death bed visions.

3. Indications of evidence based on near-death experiences.

4. Indications of evidence based on out-of-body experiences.

5. Indications of evidence based on mediumship.

6. Indications of evidence based on automatic writing.

7. Indications of evidence based on materialization.

8. Indications of evidence based on apparitions.

9. Indications of evidence based on cross-correspondences.

The Indications of Survival

10. Indications of evidence based on possession.

11. Indications of evidence based on reincarnation.

12. Indications of evidence based on electronic voice phenomena.

13. Indications of evidence based on the fact that energy/matter are indestructible.

14. Indications of evidence based on the fact that some of the greatest minds in history have either been open to the possibility of survival or totally committed.

15. Indications of evidence based on the fact that God has a definite plan for each life.

16. Indications of evidence based on the Bible.

17. Indications of evidence based on the nature and character of God.

18. Indications of evidence based on Christ's resurrection.

19. Indications of evidence based on the purpose and grand design of the universe.

20. Indications of evidence based on the nature of man.

21. Indications of evidence based on natural law.

22. Indications of evidence based on the fact that life would be absurd unless consciousness continued beyond physical death.

23. Indications of evidence based on our need to become whole persons.

24. Indications of evidence based on man's intuition.

25. Indications of evidence based on man's aspirations.

26. Indications of evidence based on universality of belief.

27. Indications of evidence based on man's innate drives and the need for satisfaction.

Indications of Evidence Based on the Consistency of Reports Concerning the Same Experiences.

Gifted sensitives, working independently and separated by many years, and who have been in contact with those who have predeceased them, exhibit remarkable consistency in their journals and writings.

Examples would be the information they received concerning growth and development on the other side; that as we sow we reap; that the next state of consciousness is remarkably similar to what we experienced in the physical state; that we create by the powers of the mind; that our characters, our personalities, aren't suddenly changed in the twinkling of an eye after we make the transition. The list is long.

Such repetition and substantial agreement world-wide might not be considered valid from the empirical standpoint, but it points in the direction of truth.

Indications of Evidence Based on Death-Bed Visions

Persons on the brink or threshold of death are frequently greeted by close friends or relatives who have predeceased them. They are welcomed as they are about to begin the next step in their spiritual adventure. Occasionally, in death-bed visions, the one who is about to make the transition will see and speak with a loved one whom he did not know had died.

In his provocative and stimulating book, *The Supreme Adventure*, Robert Crookall speaking on the subject, notes that "A person who is in the course of a natural transition is said, in communications from 'beyond,' to send out a kind of 'call' to friends and relatives who have 'gone before.' This 'call' sometimes consists of deliberate and conscious thoughts; sometimes it is more or less instinctive and subconscious."[1]

In the case of sudden death, as a result of an accident, war or suicide, there may not be a welcoming committee, because loved ones on the other side haven't had time to prepare. However, this does not mean the individual is outside the circle of God's love.

In *Death-Bed Visions*, by Sir William Barrett, there is an account of such an incident related by Dr. E. H. Plumptre in the *Spectator*, August 26, 1882:

"The mother of one of the foremost thinkers and theologians of our time was lying on her death-bed in the April of 1854. She had been for some days in a state of almost complete unconsciousness. A short time before her death, the words came from her lips, 'There they are, all of them - William and Elizabeth, and Emma and Anne;' then, after a pause, 'and Priscilla too.' William was a son who had died in infancy, and whose name had never for years passed the mother's lips. Priscilla had died two days before, but her death, though known to the family, had not been reported to her."[2]

This revealing death-bed experience, one of many reported over the years, would appear to me to be irrefutable evidence for continuation of personality following physical death.

Indications of Evidence Based on Near-Death Experiences (N.D.E.)

A near-death experience is when a person has been pronounced clinically dead (no heartbeat, respiration or other vital signs) and has been resuscitated or brought back from the threshold of death. The *Chicago Daily News* reported a dramatic near-death experience involving a Hammond, Indiana man. Doctors pronounced him dead following an appendectomy. He soon proved them wrong.

He said, "My recollections were of passing through a tunnel and arriving on the brink of something. I seemed reluctant to go on. I had a feeling of great serenity and a slight disappointment at not being able or willing to go on. I was very puzzled about the deaths of people close to me.

He said that while "dead" he found himself asking why a brother-in-law, a young man, had died in a wartime plane crash.

"I asked why it had to be," he wrote. "And it was explained to me by some entity I can't identify. I remember saying over and over: 'Of course, of course, it had to be.'

"It was a revelation to me, as if the pieces of a jigsaw puzzle were all magically fitted together.

"The thing I have trouble explaining is that the reasons (for the brother-in-law's death) were joyful reasons and a great feeling of relief and serenity came over me.

"Since this experience, I have never feared death."[3]

While such experiences have been noted throughout history, this phenomenon was vividly brought to the attention of the public by Dr. Raymond Moody, Jr., a philosopher and medical doctor. In 1975, his book, *Life After Life*, was published and stimulated wide interest.

Dr. Elisabeth Kubler-Ross, an M.D. and prominent thanatologist, had prepared the way for Moody's revelations with her professional investigations into the near-death experience. A more scientific and systematic analysis has since been conducted by researchers Karlis Osis, Erlendur Haraldsson and Kenneth Ring.

An N.D.E. is usually precipitated by a crisis situation, such as a severe accident, an illness, heart attack, attempted suicide, near drownings or other life-threatening occurrences. It is a brink-of-death circumstance.

Persons who have undergone a near-death experience report remarkably consistent features, with variations depending on the individual. In a pamphlet published by the *International Association for Near-Death Studies, Inc.* the principal components of the N.D.E. are given:

1. A feeling of extreme ease, peace and well-being.
2. Finding oneself outside of one's physical body.
3. Floating or drifting through a dark tunnel or passageway.
4. Perceiving a brilliant golden or golden-yellow light which seems to radiate warmth, love and unconditional acceptance.
5. A telepathic and non-judgmental encounter with a "presence" or "being of light."
6. A panoramic life review.
7. Entering into a transcendent realm of almost indescribable beauty.
8. Meeting with (deceased) loved ones or spiritual guides who inform the individual that he must return to earthly life.[4]

Those who have been resuscitated frequently tell of their reluctance to return to their physical bodies. Attitudes have been changed, moral and spiritual values enhanced, and their capacity to love has been immeasurably increased.

In my opinion, the near-death experience gives credible evidence of survival.

Indications of Evidence Based on Out-of-Body Experiences

Such experiences occur when the finer spiritual body separates from the denser physical body, usually, but not always as a result of a crisis situation.

The two bodies interpenetrate while the physical body exists. They are connected by a silver cord, which is mentioned in the Old Testament Book of Ecclesiastes 12:6: "Remember him-before the silver cord is severed."

When the cord is severed, the two bodies are permanently separated. There isn't any more pronounced evidence for survival than the out-of-body experience.

D. Scott Rogo, who authored the book *The Welcoming Silence*, states emphatically that, "...The crucial point in survival evidence is the out-of-body experience."[5]

One of my former students, who had an out-of-body experience, relates the following incident: "During an illness, I distinctly remember hovering over my husband (on a ship somewhere in the Pacific) and watching as the radio operator gave him the message that I had died. I watched my poor grief-stricken husband cry and yell; every sailor trying to calm and ease his pain and grief. Then I remember myself crying and saying, 'I can't stand to see Andy hurt and cry; he needs me and loves me.' I guess that it was then the silver cord got straightened out and God sent me back to continue in this beautiful world."

Sylvan Muldoon, who had his share of out-of-body travel, testifies to his belief in survival as a result of his experiences: "For my part, had a book on immortality never been written, had a lecture on 'survival' never been uttered, had I never witnessed a seance or visited a medium; in fact, had no one else in the whole world ever suspected 'life after death,' I should still believe implicitly that I am immortal—for I have experienced the projection of the astral body."[6]

This would provide dramatic proof of the two bodies of man; the physical and the spiritual. Furthermore, an out-of-body experience testifies to the fact that the spiritual body can separate from its earthly counterpart.

Indications of Evidence Based On Mediumship

This category provides the most substantial and common confirmatory data concerning spirit survival.

A medium, or sensitive, is a link, a channel, a telephone line, permitting conversation with those who are temporarily in the physical body with those who are in the permanent spiritual body.

For the sake of convenience, mediumship is usually placed in two categories: *Physical mediumship* is primarily associated with the attempt to produce physical phenomena such as the movement of objects, table-tilting, psychic photography, levitation and rappings.

An excellent example of physical mediumship is the Biblical incident where Jesus walked on the water: "During the fourth watch of the night Jesus went out to them, walking on the lake..." (Matthew 14:25).

Mental mediumship is closely associated with communication between two worlds; the forming of mental impressions of what is seen and heard from spirit communicators. The sensitive is usually in a state of mild or deep trance. Given the proper conditions, the so-called dead communicate through mediums. Mental mediumship over the years has been the most productive as far as proof of survival is concerned.

While fraud and trickery have always plagued mediumship, all it takes is one authentic example of communication to prove the point. As mentioned previously, it is precisely as William James has said: "...If you wish to upset the law that all crows are black, you must not seek to show that no crows are; it is enough if you prove one single crow to be white..."[7]

Representative of mental mediumship are clairvoyance, clairaudience, psychometry and trance communications.

An honest and open-minded study of the Bible will quickly reveal several striking examples of genuine mediumship. I Samuel, Chapter 28 is especially illustrative. The medium is the Woman of Endor (not the Witch of Endor as some translations state). The two other major participants in this drama are Saul and Samuel. Saul was having real problems and sought the advice of the "dead" Samuel. The Woman of Endor was the intermediary and made contact. A spirited conversation followed between Saul and Samuel. The results were not happy for Saul as you will note when you study the Scripture. This passage clearly indicates the ability of this remarkable woman to make contact with one who was living in another dimension.

One of the most revealing incidents of mediumship in the Bible takes place on the Mount of Transfiguration and is found in Matthew, Chapter 17. The participants are Jesus, Peter, James and John. Jesus was the sensitive, but the other three were possessed of great psychic power also. The Bible plainly states "...Just then there appeared before them Moses and Elijah talking with Jesus." This is an explicit and as concrete an example as you can find of communication or channeling. This is mediumship at its best. And, it is Biblical.

The importance of mediumship, with its many facets, cannot be overestimated in any consideration of evidence for survival.

Direct Voice Mediumship has been productive of highly veridical testimony concerning survival. In the presence of a trance medium, a spirit communicator speaks, but the voice is independent of the medium. Occasionally an aluminum trumpet is used to amplify the communication. These independent voices are so exact in tone, expression and mannerism that it is difficult to deny the identity of the communicator. In some instances, more than one voice can be heard.

Direct voice mediums of the past include: George Valiantine, Gladys Osborne Leonard, Margery Crandon, David Duguid and D. D. Home.

Scripture is expressive of Direct Voice Mediumship as you will note in the following passages:

1. Genesis 21:17-18 — (The Old Testament incident of Hagar and Ishmael): "God heard the boy crying, and the angel of God called to Hagar from heaven and said to her, 'What is the matter, Hagar? Do not be afraid; God has heard the boy crying as he lies there. Lift the boy up and take him by the hand, for I

will make him into a great nation.'"

2. Exodus, Chapter 3 — (The familiar story of Moses and the burning bush) God calls Moses for a particular service; to go back to his captive people and to lead them out of the land of Egypt.

3. I Samuel 3:2-14 — (The Lord calls the boy Samuel). He is called to be a prophet and the downfall of Eli is revealed to the boy. This is very clear evidence of direct voice mediumship.

4. Mark 1:9-11 — (A decisive moment in Jesus' life when he was baptized). "At that time Jesus came from Nazareth in Galilee and was baptized by John in the Jordan. As Jesus was coming up out of the water, he saw heaven being torn open and the Spirit descending on him like a dove. And a voice came from heaven: 'You are my Son, whom I love; with you I am well pleased.'" This is an outstanding example of direct voice.

5. Mark 9:7 — (Here God gives a command to the disciples. The voice was heard during the climax of the Transfiguration). "Then a cloud appeared and enveloped them, and a voice came from the cloud: 'This is my Son, whom I love. Listen to him!'"

It should be noted, and this is important, that communication between God and man was direct in those ancient days. Evidence for this is abundant in many Old Testament passages. This is especially true in the account of Moses' encounter with the burning bush. Exodus 3:4 states: "When the Lord saw that he had gone over to look, God called to him from within the bush, 'Moses! Moses!'" And Moses said, "Here I am." In order to get the full impact, read the entire chapter.

Time and time again in those early Old Testament books we find such passages as, "Then the Lord spoke to Moses..." The lawgiver would reply. So it was a two-way conversation.

We have lost this marvelous ability because of our disobedience and the chaotic clutter of our lives with material possessions as well as our selfish response to life. While prayer and meditation aren't withinthe purview of this book, it would certainly be one foot in the door in recapturing the vitality, signs and wonders of those early years.

Indications of Evidence through Automatic Writing

This is another facet of mediumship that has produced serious evidence of survival.

This type of writing is done by an individual without conscious awareness or muscular control. It is, however, difficult to determine whether the hand doing the writing is controlled by persons in the discarnate state, or whether it is a product of the writer's subconscious mind.

Automatism can manifest in many ways, such as involuntary writing, painting, drawing and speaking. Painting and drawings are often done with unbelievable speed and frequently in great detail.

Writing has appeared upside down, perpendicular, in barely legible words, miniscule childish scrawl, or in beautiful script. Foreign languages have also been produced.

It is quite evidential that some automatic writing has displayed knowledge and ability far beyond that possessed by the automatist. In some cases, genius was visibly evident in the output.

Harriet Beecher Stowe claims to have written *Uncle Tom's Cabin* while in semi-trance. Dickens did not live to complete his novel *The Mystery of Edwin Drood*, so American T. P. James finished the work automatically. William Blake wrote his poem *Jerusalem* by automatic writing. Victor Hugo and Goethe also claimed to have created works using this style of mediumship.

In 1972, my wife and I were guests of English medium, George Daisley, in Santa Barbara, California. While we were busy with his autobiography, a message was received through him from Bishop James A. Pike. The brief paragraph, commending our work on the book, was written backwards and could only be read by holding it up to a mirror.

The Ouija board, a form of automatic writing, has been productive of books, poems and other literary expressions.

What appears to be authentic communication from the other side is found in the writings of St. Louis housewife, Mrs. Pearl Curran. Through the inspiration of discarnate Patience Worth, a 17th century young English girl, Mrs. Curran composed a remarkable array of books and poems initially through the use of the ouija board. Her books include *The Sorry Tale, Hope Trueblood, Light from Beyond,* and *The Pot Upon the Wheel.* With

Patience Worth, Mrs. Curran wrote over a million and a half words from 1913 to 1937. Many of her vocal critics agree that her writing was far beyond her capabilities.

Did the subconscious mind of Pearl Curran contribute to her literary output, or was Patience Worth, in spirit, responsible for these books, poems, epigrams and aphorisms? *The Case of Patience Worth*, by Walter Franklin Prince, gives a lucid account of this unique contribution to the history of automatic writing.

In Anita M. Muhl's descriptive book, *Automatic Writing*, she relates a rather humorous example of such writing. It seems that an Egyptologist discovered a jar of castor oil in an ancient tomb in which a flea had been preserved. The Egyptologist who made the discovery penned the following bit of doggerel employing automatic writing. It is entitled, *In Memorium*:

> "3000 years ago there was a
> little flea
> Who saw a jar of castor oil
> and thot it was the sea
> How now, quoth he, how fine,
> Tis just the place to rest
> I'm weary of the wine and of
> the song and jest
> So in this noble set I'll
> let myself recline
> My arid tongue I'll wet and
> rest myself supine
> And anon his mamma
> a-hopping through the air
> Descried her youngest wee
> one crouched in deep despair
> She came too late-he sipped
> and fell into the pool
> A-shouting as he did so,
> 'Tis great to be a fool.'"[8]

In September of 1973, my wife and I had the pleasure of visiting with Ruth Montgomery in Cuernavaca, Mexico. You'll remember she is the author of the best selling books *A Gift of Prophecy* and *A Search for the Truth*.

Much of Ruth's writing has been the product of automatic

writing, such as *Companions Along the Way*, *The World Before* and my favorite, *A World Beyond*.

Eileen and I asked Ruth about techniques she used in her automatic writing and how she approached it. One of our questions was, "Do you have a particular discipline in your writing?"

She said that "For the automatic writing, it is the same time every morning, 8:30 a.m. I warn readers to set the same time every day. Fifteen minutes is spent in neck and breathing exercises of the Cayce kind, then a chant and a brief meditation. That puts me in the alpha state and with a little prayer for protection, I flip on the electric typewriter. I sit with my eyes closed and it goes a mile a minute. My fingers can hardly keep up. It begins, 'Ruth, this is Lily, Art and the Group.'"

Psychic Arthur Ford, who made the transition in 1971, is her principal communicator.

An extensive account of Ruth's automatic writing is found in her autobiography *Herald of the New Age*.

In any consideration of evidential material for survival of consciousness, automatic writing must be considered a prime contributor.

Indications of Evidence Based on Materialization

A rare form of mediumship, materialization occurs when a discarnate, or spirit entity, clothes itself with matter (ectoplasm). It is gelatinous in appearance and flows from the orifices of a materialization sensitive. Discarnates are able to shape or mould the substance producing either a partial or full figure. Probably 90% or more of what purports to be materialization is nonsense or simply fraud. However, it takes one authentic case to prove the point. When genuine, there isn't any question that consciousness survives physical death.

Physicist William Crookes' major interest in the paranormal centered in mediumship. His intense interest in sensitive Florence Cook and the materialized Katie King opened new avenues of investigation for Crookes.

In the early 1870's, photographs were obtained of the materializations, and in his book *Phenomena of Spiritualism*, he remarks, "One of the most interesting of the pictures is one in which I am standing by the side of Kate; she has her bare feet upon a particular part of the floor. Afterwards I dressed Miss Cook like Katie, placed her and myself in exactly the same position, and we were photographed by the same cameras, placed exactly as in the other experiment, and illuminated by the same light. When these two pictures are placed over each other, the two photographs of myself coincide exactly as regards stature, etc., but Katie is half a head taller than Miss Cook, and looks a big woman in comparison with her. In the breadth of her face, in many of the pictures, she differs essentially in size from her medium, and the photographs show several other points of difference...I have the most absolute certainty that Miss Cook and Katie are two separate individuals as far as their bodies are concerned..."[9]

Scriptural accounts of materialization are equally as graphic and fascinating.

1. Genesis 18:2. Three angelic visitors appear to Abraham: "...Abraham looked up and saw three men standing nearby..."

2. Judges 13.3. "...the angel of the Lord appeared to her and said..."

3. I Samuel 28:11-12. "...Then the woman asked, 'Whom shall I bring up for you?' 'Bring up Samuel,' he said. When the woman saw Samuel, she cried out at the top of her voice and said to Saul, 'Why have you deceived me? You are Saul!'"

4. Job 4:15-16. "...A spirit glided past my face...but I could not tell what it was. A form stood before my eyes..."

5. Matthew 28:1-8. Jesus materialized in the garden alongside the tomb.

6. Mark 9:2-8. The Transfiguration. Moses and Elijah, long departed, materialize. Other than materializing, this passage proves that the so-called dead can communicate with those in the physical body.

7. Luke 24:13-30. Jesus materialized to two men on the road to

Emmaus.

8. John 20:19. "On the evening of that first day of the week, when the disciples were together, with the doors locked for fear of the Jews, Jesus came and stood among them..."

9. John 21.1. Jesus materialized on the lakeshore to the men who were fishing.

The physical characteristics in materialization are nothing short of amazing. The figure is not only seen but can talk, walk around and can be photographed. It has on occasion been touched, and in the case of William Crookes, Katie King, the materialized spirit, allowed him to hug her. The heart beats, a pulse is evident, there is a body temperature and blood flows through the materialized visitor's veins. The breathing spirit is completely life-like in a temporary physical body.

It would appear, in studying the phenomena of materialization, that these spirit forms almost always interact with individuals for purposes of identification. What better proof of continuation of consciousness than to appear so life-like.

Prominent materialization sensitives of the past include Florence Cook, Eva. C. (Marthe Beraud), D. D. Home, Mme. D'Esperance, Eusapia Palladino and Margery Crandon.

Indications of Evidence
Based on Cross-Correspondences

This evidence consists of fragmentary messages from the other side received through more than one sensitive all of whom are sitting in different places at different times. When such fragments are compared, a meaningful pattern emerges. Cross-correspondences are similar to a jig-saw puzzle. It is only when all of the pieces are in place that a complete picture appears.

The instigator of cross-correspondences is said to be F. W. H. Myers who passed into spirit in 1901. He was a classical scholar, so when these independent messages were assembled, there were numerous references and allusions to classical literature. They were extremely difficult to decipher unless you were schooled in the classics. Examples well worth studying are: *Hope, Star and Browning;* the *Lethe;* and *The Ear of Dionysius.*

It is said, and with very good reason, that cross-correspondences furnish remarkable and convincing evidence for survival.

Indications of Evidence Based on Apparitions

An apparition is a vivid and life-like appearance of a person, living or dead, in his or her spiritual body. The specter usually has a motive and has been known to engage in conversation. The apparition is recognized and is frequently seen by very close friends or relatives because an emotional bond exists.

G. N. M. Tyrrell in his book *Apparitions,* divides them into four main classes:

1. "Experimental cases, in which the agent has deliberately tried to make his apparition visible to a particular percipient.

2. "Cases in which a recognized apparition is seen, heard or felt at the time when the person represented by the apparition is undergoing some crisis.

3. "Cases in which a recognized apparition is seen or heard so long after the death of the person represented by the apparition that no coincidence with any crisis, such as the death of the person, can be supposed.

4."Ghosts, or apparitions, which habitually haunt certain places." [10]

The Society for Psychical Research's meaningful *Census of Hallucinations,* released in 1889, illustrated the fact that apparitions occur in moments of great crisis and emotional upheaval. Tyrrell felt that the "crisis apparition" was telepathic in origin.

Dwayne Whitaker, a resident of Roswell, New Mexico, related the following personal experience that he had while stationed with the U. S. Army on the Island of Guam.

"It was the year 1952, and one evening I was standing on the wing of an airplane. The escape hatches of the plane were open. Suddenly, I saw my dad crawl out of the main escape hatch and walk toward me. He was dressed in blue jeans and a blue T shirt. He was also wearing the silly little cap he always wore. He looked hot and dusty and had chaff all over his clothes. He appeared very tired. "Stunned, I asked him what he was doing in Guam nearly 10,000 miles from home? He didn't answer me. He just smiled; it was a peaceful smile. We shook hands and I felt his hand in mine. I saw him just as well as I see you. Another plane was taking off, so I turned my head briefly to watch. When I turned back, he was gone. I knew right then and there that my dad had died.

"I received the message of my dad's death through the American Red Cross. I told them I already knew. They asked me how I knew. I told them 'I just know.'

"I immediately left for home, but arrived too late for the funeral. I asked mom what dad was wearing when he died. She described the clothes, and they were the same he was wearing when I saw him on that airplane wing in Guam.

"My mother said my dad had been putting up hay and had just pitched his last fork. He took his hanky out of his pocket and wiped his forehead. When he put it back in his pocket, he said, 'This is the last load I'm ever going to pitch.' He fell off the wagon and the doctor said he was dead before he hit the ground. He had died at exactly the same time I had seen him on the plane's wing in Guam."

Several more important points concerning apparitions should be mentioned:

1. Apparitions have been seen by more than one individual; that is, collectively.

2. It should again be emphasized that apparitions can be of the living as well as the dead. The latter occurs when a person, or agent, knowingly attempts to project himself to another person.

3. Not only persons but animals have appeared apparitionally.

4. Apparitions can appear substantial and completely life-like. They may be clothed in familiar garments and other recognizable belongings.

Apparitions give credible evidence to the statement that physical death is but a gateway to further new and exciting adventures.

Indications of Evidence Based on Possession

Possession is the intrusion of an individual's personality by either an earthbound discarnate or some other foreign entity.

Possession by such entities is genuine. History is explicit and detailed in this respect, and the idea or concept is as old as anything narrated in our history books. Ancient cultures were saturated with reports of possession. Shamans, medicine men and spiritual leaders confirm this. Writers of ancient days, such as Plato, Socrates, Aristotle, Plutarch and others refer to demonic influences and possessing entities.

The Old and New Testaments readily acknowledge the existence of possessing entities. Note I Samuel 16:23:

"Whenever the spirit from God came upon Saul, David would take his harp and play. Then relief would come to Saul; he would feel better, and the evil spirit would leave him."

And in the New Testament: Matthew 10:1:

"And he called his twelve disciples to him and gave them authority to drive out evil spirits and to heal every disease and sickness."

Mark 1:39 is another example of possession:

"...So he traveled throughout Galilee, preaching in their synagogues and driving out demons."

In Luke 8:27-33 is yet another illustration:

"When Jesus stepped ashore, he was met by a demon-possessed man from the town. For a long time this man had not worn clothes or lived in a house, but had lived in the tombs. When he saw Jesus, he cried out and fell at his feet, shouting at the top of his voice, 'What do you want with me, Jesus, Son of the most high God? I beg you, don't torture me!' For Jesus had commanded the evil spirit to come out of the man. Many times it had seized him, and though he was chained hand and foot and kept under guard, he had broken his chains and had been driven by the demon into solitary places.

"Jesus asked him, 'What is your name?'

"'Legion,' he replied, because many demons had gone into him. And they begged him repeatedly not to order them to go into the abyss.

"A large herd of pigs was feeding there on the hillside. The demons begged Jesus to let them go into them, and he gave them permission. When the demons came out of the man, they went into the pigs and the herd rushed down the steep bank into the lake and was drowned."

Another pointed and dramatic Scriptural account of possession is found in Mark 9:17-2. Here Jesus cures the epileptic boy. This is a most revealing event and is well worth reading in your favorite Bible translation.

I am convinced, as a result of many years of research into psychic matters, that Dr. Carl A. Wickland is correct when he says, "...The spiritual world and the physical world are constantly intermingling..." [11]

This would suggest that earthbound entities or spirits are active within close proximity of our earth and exert strong influence in the lives of those who have very little control over their daily affairs. They gratify their former earthly desires by proxy, being unable to satisfy them in their new condition. These undeveloped spirits, bewildered and confused, attach themselves to the auras of those still in the physical body.

With the evidence available concerning possession and obsession, it would appear that it speaks strongly in favor of survival. Obsession, it should be noted, is discarnate influence in human life, rather than an actual inner invasion and personality disruption. One can only discern the difference by observing the behavior patterns.

For further study, I would recommend the book *Watseka* by David St. Clair. This interesting volume tells the story of 13-year-old Lurancy Vennum and 19-year-old Mary Roff who possessed Lurancy for many weeks. This thoroughly researched case is stunning and highly evidential. Also, especially worth reading is *Thirty Years Among the Dead*, by Carl Wickland.

Indications of Evidence Based on Reincarnation

This is rebirth of the soul in human flesh; the belief that man must experience many lifetimes before he reaches spiritual perfection.

Do not confuse reincarnation with transmigration. The latter implies the rebirth of the soul into lower forms of life.

Integral to reincarnation is the doctrine of karma; cause and effect. You reap what you sow. You have certain lessons to learn, and future incarnations are dependent upon your behavior in this lifetime. Your conduct is the key. There is good and bad karma, and the ideal is to avoid the bad. Such things as hate and dishonesty merit retribution in future incarnations, while acts of compassion and charity reap rewards for the doer in a future lifetime.

Reincarnation purportedly is a handy explanation for all the suffering and injustice so evident everywhere, such as crippling illnesses, poverty and widespread starvation.

Memories of past lives, discovered through hypnotic regression, is a prime method for seeking the truth of rebirth.

Studies in the field have proved productive, and the leading researcher and renouned authority is Dr. Ian Stevenson, head of the Division of Parapsychology, Department of Behavioral Medicine and Psychiatry, University of Virginia. His book, *Twenty Cases Suggestive of Reincarnation*, is a classic in the field of reincarnation, and his investigations have attracted wide attention especially among professionals. The cases of Shanti Devi in India and Corliss Chotkin, Jr., in southeastern Alaska, are among the most celebrated.

Child prodigies are supposedly explained by reincarnation. Composer Wolfgang Mozart, from his earliest years, exhibited remarkable talent. When he was three, he was writing music and before he was six, stories abound of his absolutely amazing ability. Child mathematical and musical geniuses, and astoundingly gifted linguists are all credited with being the products of rebirth.

Do certain passages of Scripture give credence to reincarnation? Devout believers feel strongly that they do. Passages usually cited are:

1. Matthew 16:13-1. "When Jesus came to the region of Caesarea Philippi, he asked his disciples, 'Who do people say the Son of Man is?'

"They replied, 'Some say John the Baptist; others say Elijah; and still others, Jeremiah or one of the prophets.'"

2. Matthew 17:10-1. "The disciples asked him, 'Why then do the teachers of the law say that Elijah must come first?'

"Jesus replied, 'To be sure, Elijah comes and will restore all things. But I tell you, Elijah has already come, and they did not recognize him, but have done to him everything they wished. In the same way the Son of Man is going to suffer at their hands.' Then the disciples understood that he was talking to them about John the Baptist."

3. John 3:. "In reply Jesus declared, 'I tell you the truth, no one can see the kingdom of God unless he is born again.'"

4. John 9:1-. "As he went along, he saw a man blind from birth. His disciples asked him, 'Rabbi, who sinned, this man or his parents, that he was born blind?' 'Neither this man nor his parents sinned,' said Jesus, 'But this happened so that the work of God might be displayed in his life...'"

When we make the transition from the physical to the spiritual body, do we, following a period of self-appraisal, make our own decision as to whether we wish to reincarnate? It would seem so. Freedom of choice, operative on this side, is also a natural law on the other.

Another intriguing question is whether we choose our future parents and the circumstances under which we will live when we reincarnate.

Benjamin Franklin had the following inscribed on his tombstone:

"The body of B. Franklin,
Printer,
Like the cover of an old book,
Its contents torn out and
Stripped of its lettering & Gilding
Lies here
But the book will not be lost,
For it will as he believed
appear once more
In a new and more elegant
edition
Revised and corrected
By the author"[12]

I have found it difficult at this point in time to include reincarnation in my personal world view. (My reincarnation friends tell me I didn't believe it the first time I was here!) However, I consider it one of the options given to us, allowing those who so believe to inherit all the promises of God's Kingdom. Reincarnation gives assurance of eternal life and this is what is important. My mind continues to be open on the subject.

There is much information that is highly suggestive of reincarnation but it is still a theory. Whatever our opinion, reincarnation must always be included in any research and discussion concerning survival. It must never be forgotten that two-thirds of the world's population believe in rebirth and this is very significant.

Indications of Evidence Based on Electronic Voice Phenomena

This novel and interesting method of communicating with discarnates is accomplished through the use of a tape recorder. Pioneers in this field include Attila Von Szalay, Friedrich Jurgenson and Konstantin Raudive. The voices heard are extremely faint, fragmented, fleeting and often in foreign languages. It is quite possible that voices on tape provide another link in the chain of evidence for survival.

Those of you with an adventuresome turn of mind, set up

your tape recorder in a very quiet place. Invite any entity to communicate directly into your waiting tape recorder. By way of introduction, you can ask pertinent questions and invite a response. There may be anxious moments of waiting in silence for that reply, but you might join the ranks of those who have actually heard a voice on tape. It does require patience and time.

A breakthrough of breath-taking proportions in electronic voice phenomena may have occurred in the work of the Metascience Foundation in Franklin, North Carolina. In April 1982, George W. Meek, an engineer and inventor, announced that he, along with co-workers, had achieved success in establishing a two-way communication with several individuals on the other side. The instrument used was an electromagnetic-etheric apparatus called Spiricom. Caution should be exercized in this matter, because the reliability of Meek's work has come under some criticism.

Author John G. Fuller has written the story of George Meek and Spiricom in his book, *The Ghost of 29 Megacycles*. It is worth reading for an overview of the project. Only time will reveal its authenticity.

Indications of Evidence Based on the Fact that Energy/Matter are Indestructible

This is one of the most telling points that can be made for survival. Matter can neither be created nor destroyed according to the first law of thermodynamics. But it does change form. The Rev. Deane Starr, a Minister of the Unitarian-Universalist Church, speaks to this fact: "For me, the awareness that I am composed of eternal, indestructible matter/energy is a source of never-ending delight and amazement. To look at one's hands and to realize that the elements that compose them have been around forever and will be around forever boggles the mind. And the fact that they will eventually disintegrate, that they will eventually decompose to become parts of new entities, becomes a matter of no great moment."[13]

Matter is indestructible, so isn't it logical to say that consciousness survives the death experience? The created order wouldn't make any sense if it didn't. The Apostle Paul alludes to this fact by saying, "...Listen, I tell you a mystery: we will not all sleep, but we will all be changed..." (I Corinthians 15:51)

Marcus Aurelius in his *Meditations* talks about loss as nothing else than change.[14]

During the winter months in Roswell, New Mexico, I tend our wood stove and periodically remove the ashes that accumulate. The logs that burn so cheerfully and provide warmth are soon reduced to ashes. The former logs have now been transformed to another state. Fallen trees disintegrate in the forest; they rot and nourish the soil. Nature knows only conservation, not death or loss. Surely we are worth more to God than the lower forms of His creation.

In summary, note the incisive words of Charles Tweedale in his book, *Man's Survival after Death*:

"Matter is eternal and indestructible; space stretching out to infinity and time rolling on to eternity are everlasting and indestructible; suns and systems change and decay, only to be renewed. Is human personality inferior to these great entities?... Is the personal inferior to the impersonal?"[15]

Indications of Evidence Based on the Fact that Some of the Greatest Minds in History Have Either Been Open to the Possibility of Survival or Totally Committed

Many highly intelligent and exceptionally qualified persons, of great integrity, were and are involved in psychical research. Some have been scientifically trained and oriented. Their work and person bear thoughtful study and research.

In looking to past activity, Arthur Koestler in *Roots of Coincidence*, points out that the character of the Society for Psychical Research, organized in London in 1882, was established in consideration of several of its past presidents. Among them were: "...three Nobel Laureates, ten Fellows of the Royal Society, one Prime Minister and a galaxy of professors, mostly physicists and philosophers."[16]

Individuals of enormous creative energy and talent, caught up in the excitement of the unknown, made highly significant contributions to the advancement of psychical research. Their names are honored and respected. Before mentioning some of the prominent of past years, I first want to place before you a listing of some of our contemporaries; a few keep us informed through the written word; others are primarily researchers; some teach, while there are those who are skilled in all areas of the discipline.

Among them are: Karlis Osis, Stanley Krippner, Ramakrishna Rao, Ian Stevenson, John Beloff, William Roll, Charles Tart, Russell Targ, Harold Putthoff, Gertrude Schmeidler, Helmut Schmidt, Harold Sherman, Thelma Moss, Edgar Mitchell, Milan Ryzl, Barbara Brown, Hans Bender, Raymond Moody, Jr., Elisabeth Kubler-Ross, D. Scott Rogo, Kenneth Ring, Susy Smith, Raymond Bayless, Brad Steiger, Paul Beard, Walter and Mary Jo Uphoff, Lawrence LeShan, Rex Stanford, George Meek, Allen Spraggett, Ruth Montgomery, Larry and Valere Althouse, Arthur Berger, Susan Blackmore, Brian Inglis, Leslie Price, Colin Wilson, Alan Vaughan, Antony Flew, Raynor Johnson, Hans Holzer, Martin Ebon, Dick Sutphen, John Fuller, Jule Eisenbud, Michael Perry and Alan Gauld.

In past years, the roll call of outstanding pathfinders in the field of psychical research is made up of some rather remarkable individuals. To name some of the most outstanding:

Emanuel Swedenborg (1688-1772), Alfred Russel Wallace (1823-1913), Sir William Crookes (1832-1919), Henry Sidgwick (1838-1900), William James (1842-1910), Camille Flammarion (1842-1925), F. W. H. Myers (1843-1901), Arthur Lang (1844-1912), Sir William Barrett (1844-1925), Eleanor Mildred Balfour Sidgwick (1845-1936), Edmund Gurney (1847-1888), Thomas Edison (1847-1931), Arthur James Balfour (1848-1930), Charles Richet (1850-1935), Sir Oliver Lodge (1851-1940), James Hervey Hyslop (1854-1920), Richard Hodgson (1855-1905), Sigmund Freud (1856-1939), Sir Arthur Conan Doyle (1859-1930), Henri Bergson (1859-1941), Lawrence P. Jacks (1860-1955), F.C.S. Schiller (1864-1937), William Mc Dougall (1871-1938), Carl Jung (1875-1961), Upton Sinclair (1878-1968), Curt John Ducasse (1881-1969), C. D. Broad (1887-1971), Hornell Hart (1888-1967), Robert Crookall (1890-?), Gardner Murphy (1895-1979), and J. B. Rhine (1895-1989).

Indications of Evidence Based on the Fact that God Has a Definite Plan for Each Life

One very wise individual speaks of life as a divine appointment because it was God who introduced us into the mysteries and wonders of His creation.

Each of us is a part of God's grand design and the role we play, major or minor, is supremely important. Much depends upon our lifelong faithfulness to this plan, so that ultimately we will be able to say with the Apostle Paul, "...I have fought the good fight, I have finished the race, I have kept the faith...." (II Timothy 4:7)

Just as there is a universal plan that gives history its purpose and meaning, so it is with the individual.

Paul Tournier, the Swiss psychiatrist and theologian, feels that God's plan is fulfilled not only through obedient, inspired men but also through their errors and sins. So all of life's events and occurrences, of whatever nature, tragic or noble, are securely imbedded in this master plan.

In no way am I talking about determinism or predestination. Free will is never crossed out or absent from any phase of this divine plan, and indeed it prevails not only on this side but on the other side of physical death as well.

Just as a jigsaw puzzle is incomplete unless that last solitary piece is put in place, so it is for us. Each of us is unique and blessed with talent, and God utilizes it as part of his vast master plan. Without your particular contribution the mosaic is incomplete. The artist's palette is resplendent with many colors and each finds its unique place on the canvas.

We are supremely important in the Creator's marvelous plan. In fact, we are partners. Witness the words of Matthew 10:29-31: "...Are not two sparrows sold for a penny? Yet not one of them will fall to the ground apart from the will of your Father. And even the very hairs of your head are all numbered. So don't be afraid; you are worth more than many sparrows."

How comforting it is to recall to mind that we are created in God's image and are made "...a little lower than the heavenly beings and crowned...with glory and honor." (Psalm 8, verse 5)

St. Augustine in his *Confessions* succinctly tells us the steps of a man are ordered by the Lord.

There is a purpose for everything that happens in your life because it is an integral part of your personal blueprint.

Marcus Aurelius reaffirms that every life is a plan of God: "Whatever may happen to you, it was prepared for you from all eternity; and the implication of causes was from eternity spinning the thread of your being, and of that which is incident to it."[17] How sustaining it is to take to heart the words of the Book of Romans that all things work together for good.

The grand design for each life, the climax of growth and development through eons of time, will bring as its ultimate end union with God. Every aspect, every nuance of His plan for us as individuals, will come to total and complete fruition. From beginning to end on all counts we will then be perfectly mature persons having borne the fruit of the Creator's master plan. Everything that God intended for us as a claimant of this plan will be fully realized. In Stainton Moses' book, *Spirit Teachings*, this grand strategy is put into these words: "...There will be a period at which progressive souls will eventually arrive, when progress has brought them to the very dwelling place of the Omnipotent, and that there they will lay aside their former state, and bask in the full light of deity, in contemplation of all the secrets of the universe."[18]

Indications of Evidence Based on the Bible

This evidence speaks of the salvation of *all*. Theologians label this universalism, which means that in the Christian sense no one is eternally lost, and that all humanity will ultimately be reconciled to God, whether in this life or on the other side. There is no time limit or place indicated.

Hell, or whatever state of discipline we may encounter on the other side, is considered temporary, redemptive and never punitive. This thought is commensurate with God's love.

There are passages in the Bible that support universalism:

1. "And all mankind will see God's salvation;" (Luke 3:6) "Suppose one of you has a hundred sheep and loses one of them. Does he not leave the ninety-nine in the open country and go after the lost sheep until he finds it?" (Luke 15:4)

2. "The true light that gives light to every man was coming into the world;" (John 1:9) "But I, when I am lifted up from the earth, will draw all men to myself." (John 12:32)

3. "He must remain in heaven until the time comes for God to restore everything, as he promised long ago through his holy prophets." (Acts 3:21)

4. "For God has bound all men over to disobedience so that he may have mercy on them all." (Romans 11:32)

5. "For as in Adam all die, so in Christ all will be made alive;" (I Corinthians 15:22) "When he has done this, then the Son himself will be made subject to him who put everything under him, so that God may be all in all." (I Corinthians 15:28)

6. "That God was reconciling the world to himself in Christ, not counting men's sins against them. And he has committed to us the message of reconciliation." (II Corinthians 5:19)

7. "...And he made known to us the mystery of his will according to his good pleasure, which he purposed in Christ, to be put into effect when the times will have reached their fulfillment – to bring all things in heaven and on earth together under one head, even Christ." (Ephesians 1:9-10)

8. "That at the name of Jesus every knee should bow, in heaven and on earth, and under the earth." (Philippians 2:10)

9. "And through him to reconcile to himself all things, whether things on earth or things in heaven." (Colossians 1:20)

10. "For the grace of God that brings salvation has appeared to all men." (Titus 2:11)

11. "The Lord is not slow in keeping his promise, as some understand slowness. He is patient with you, not wanting anyone to perish, but everyone to come to repentance." (II Peter 3:9)

Several of the Apostolic Fathers were prominent universalists, and among them were Origen and Gregory of Nyssa. The Greek Father, Clement of Alexandria, was also an advocate of universalism.

Thus, hell or whatever state of discipline exists, is essentially purgative and redemptive. All human beings will be saved however long it may take. God's purpose would be eternally frustrated if this were not so. It would mean God is not in control of His creation. There are no shadows or gray areas or qualifications in His all-encompassing love. No one ever stands outside that love, and separation, if it ever exists, is always transitory. God knows only wholeness, and His divine plan, or redemptive purposes, see humanity as a whole.

William Barclay, noted Scottish Bible expositor, and anything but a rabid liberal, gives summation to what has been said. In his fascinating book, *Spiritual Autobiography*, he shares these provocative words: "But in one thing I would go beyond strict orthodoxy – I am a convinced universalist. I believe that in the end all men will be gathered into the love of God."[19]

Indications of Evidence Based on the Nature and Character of God

God is equated with love. He is love. I John 4:8 states this very clearly. It must then follow that He cannot act contrary to His nature. His love is perfect, without imperfection.

His love is exercised in concert with His justice, but it is never punitive nor condemnatory. It cannot suffer the loss of even the most flagrant of offenders. It is part of His very nature and character that we will all eventually be totally cleansed of all dross and ungodliness.

God's graciousness, mercy and forgiveness are implements of His love. To me these attributes present striking evidence that such pure and unadulterated love is far stronger than the shackles of death.

Indications of Evidence Based on Christ's Resurrection

The Resurrection of Jesus Christ is the heart of the Christian faith. It is the cornerstone of the Gospel message; its summit. In a book, long out of print, *Man's Survival After Death*, Charles L. Tweedale reminds us: "...One cannot but be impressed by one point of difference between the Christianity of today and that set forth in the Gospels and history of the early church. In these, the Resurrection, the life after death, which is the keystone of the Gospel arch, is placed absolutely in the forefront. As exemplified in the person of Christ, it is the centre around which everything else revolves, the one fact up to which everything else leads, and to which everything is subordinated."[20]

For 2000 years the Resurrection has been heralded as proof of the survival of the life principle. Our own personal survival is not dependent upon having faith in a particular religious figure or in participating in any one religious faith, but, the Resurrection is powerful evidence for the continuation of consciousness.

What else but the fact of the Resurrection could cause such a tremendous transformation of his closest followers? Following the Crucifixion their enthusiasm waned; their hopes were crushed. But with his post-Resurrection appearances, they were ready to risk even death itself. Can anyone dispute the authenticity of the Resurrection as evidence for life after death?

Indications of Evidence Based on the Purpose and Grand Design of the Universe

There is an ultimate purpose, a grand design in the mind of God for His created order. All that He has planned for it will come to completion. While directly related to evidence based on the character and nature of God, this category of evidence speaks to the natural order of things, the rationale behind the universe; its reasonableness. Its essential qualities or characteristics do more than merely suggest that the macrocosm is moving toward its ultimate purpose, for it proclaims that death is a footnote in the larger scheme of life beyond. Theologian William Barclay puts these thoughts in this frame of reference:

"...To put this very simply, in this life man can never become what reason says he ought to become, and what he is meant to become; and therefore there must be another life so that man may complete his *telos*, his end. If ever man is to become what he is meant to be, this life is not enough."[21]

While the natural order moves toward its denouement, man will also realize a sense of completion in that he will know God in a way impossible in the physical body.

Indications of Evidence Based on the Nature of Man

We are fearfully and wonderfully made, unique and very special to God. The suggestive evidence that He has a specific plan for each human being is corroborative of the fact that we are the apex of His creation.

We are more than physical beings; we have a definite spiritual dimension. It is impossible to read the Eighth Psalm without being awed and humbled. The Psalmist, without equivocation, states that God made man little lower than the heavenly beings and crowned him with glory and honor.

Even though there are times when we feel small and insignificant, God reminds us of our stature in the midst of the spiritual order. This is cause for joy, confidence and jubilation. We are created in God's image; in His likeness. Man is a reflection of the Creator and endowed with intelligence and personality. Thus, we are spiritual beings. It is impossible to know ourselves apart from Him, and St. Augustine adds a footnote in saying, "...Thou hast made us for thyself, and our hearts are restless until they find their rest in Thee."

We are God's representatives, and have been commissioned to act as His agents; to rule and have supremacy over the created order. Who and what are we? Living souls; spirits. This is our nature and our birthright. We are destined for greatness, but only through eons of time, beyond physical death, will our true majesty and wholeness be fully revealed.

Indications of Evidence Based on Natural Law

Your survival is natural to the created order. It is an immutable law of the universe that you pass through the gates of death to continue your life's journey with full conscious awareness. Death is under the domain of natural law.

The whole of creation is orderly and governed by natural law. Nothing happens by pure chance or whim. Such laws are perfect in their operation. Agnes Sanford tells us in her book, *The Healing Light*, that "God works immutably and inexorably by law."[22]

We can say with complete and absolute assurance that when our physical bodies have served their purpose, our continuing journey is immediate and automatic.

We observe nature's laws every day. We don't have to hold our breath for fear the sun will not rise; it is automatic. From the unchanging laws which govern the movement of the heavenly bodies, the changing of the seasons, to the law of gravity, we can depend upon God's faithfulness and dependability. In my very limited knowledge of astronomy, I am totally awed by the systematic and orderly routine of the heavenly bodies. How can we possibly observe the nighttime sky and not marvel at the brilliance, the preciseness and surety of the cosmos? We witness an orderly and harmonious whole.

So the universe is law-abiding. God does not suspend His laws, intervene in His creation, to perform what we erroneously call miracles. The venerable Augustine said, "God does not act contrary to nature, but only to the order of nature known to us."

In the progression and development of our spirt, we will one day comprehend at least some, if not all, of these laws. Our present finiteness is temporary. "Now we see but a poor reflection as in a mirror; then we shall see face to face. Now I know in part; then I shall know fully, even as I am fully known..." (I Corinthians 13:12)

I am indebted to Harry Emerson Fosdick for these descriptive words: "...What is called a miracle is not a rupture of law; it is the fulfilling of a larger and higher law than we have yet understood. God's providence never has and never does involve breaking his laws; it means that we are as little acquainted with all the resources of the spiritual universe as a pebble is with the resources of a plant, and that God guides the course of events by means of laws, some of which are known to us and some unknown. Remember that natural law is nothing but man's statement of how things regularly happen, *so far as he has been able to observe them.* What looks like a miracle to man is no miracle to God. To Him it is as natural as sunrise."[23]

In this explanation of natural law, the heart of the matter is survival of human personality. There is no erasure or annihilation of personality at death; indeed the natural order precludes this. Continuance of the life force is guaranteed. This is natural law.

Indications of Evidence Based on the Fact that Life Would be Absurd Unless Consciousness Continued Beyond Physical Death

If consciousness perished with the death of the physical body, life would be preposterous and we could rightly speak of God as unjust and vindictive. Without eventual fulfillment of all of our hopes and dreams, what would be the point of it all?

Life for many has been nothing but struggle and complete frustration. Their lives have been circumscribed by abject poverty, suffering and severe discouragement. Circumstances have been beyond their ability to do anything about a contemptible situation. Many individuals have fought valiantly against hopeless odds and, through no fault of their own, have sunk into quiet desperation.

Child abuse, alcoholic parents and drug problems have prevented many children and youth from living a normal life. Adulthood for them can be one of sheer despair and hopelessness. Some have not had a chance and without the assurance of continuity of personality, life would be a caricature of what God intended.

Regardless of the many injustices we witness daily, there will be repeated opportunities to mature, develop and grow on the other side of physical death.

Indications of Evidence Based on Our Need to Become Whole Persons

To become complete, whole persons, it is essential that consciousness continue beyond the death experience. In the briefest of lifetimes we have only just begun to tap our possibilities. How tragic and unreasonable it would be that just at the point where we begin to realize a measure of maturity we are suddenly cut off like a tree that is felled by a woodsman. It doesn't make any sense and it isn't logical. We must have eternity for the realization of personhood.

Leslie R. Smith, in his book *From Sunset to Dawn*, quotes Victor Hugo: "...When I go down to the grave I must say like so many others, 'I have finished my day's work.' But I cannot say, 'I have finished my life.' My day's work will begin the next morning. The tomb is not a blind alley. It is a thoroughfare. It closes in the twilight to open in the dawn."[24]

To become our own best self is a product of the years, and it doesn't happen in four score and ten. It is a process of becoming. The realization of our potential, this ripeness of the physical, mental and spiritual, demands a time frame extending far beyond the dissolution of our physical abode.

The model of maturity is Jesus Christ. I like what Edward W. Bauman says about Jesus in his superb book, *The Life and Teaching of Jesus*, commenting on the uniqueness of Christ, "...Here is a unique revelation of God, unique in its completeness, its vividness, its authority, its influence."[25]

We have in the Nazarene not only a role model, but a classic example of wholeness and completeness of personality.

So, then, this wholeness, culminating in eventual union with the living God, represents the apex of maturity reached only through growth and personal development and extending far beyond physical death. The Apostle Paul defines wholeness this way: "...But when perfection comes, the imperfect disappears. When I was a child, I talked like a child, I thought like a child, I reasoned like a child. When I became a man, I put childish ways behind me." (I Corinthians 13:10-17)

Indications of Evidence Based on Man's Intuition

I do not need logic or reason to tell me that survival is fact; I know it intuitively. It is an inner feeling that is as convincing as any evidence arrived at through the use of the scientific method. It is something that I sense or feel, but it is extremely difficult to put into words. I just know, and this is enough for me. Intuition is affirmation of external truth even though it is highly subjective.

Like John Wesley, "My heart is strangely warmed" whenever I talk about or consider survival.

Indications of Evidence Based on Man's Aspirations

Man is the only animal that can, if he will, aspire and long for significant achievement. Call it ambition or eagerness to strive for an ideal. We cultivate a vision that totally grips us, and we climb the highest mountains until we plant the flag of victory on top.

I am writing this on July 4, 1986, the 100th birthday of our Statue of Liberty. Visualize for a moment those immigrants, who, upon seeing "The Lady" for the first time, aspired to achieve in this land where anything and everything is possible.

It is the dreamers, the visionaries, who against all odds become our writers, composers, artists, statesmen, philosophers, scientists and decision-makers. We are told to stand at the door and knock and eventually it will open wide.

None other than God is the author of these impelling aspirations and I submit this as one noteworthy category of survival evidence.

Indications of Evidence Based on Universality of Belief

This category can be labeled a corollary of intuition. Belief in an afterlife, usually intuitively felt, is thoroughly imbedded in all cultures and societies from antiquity to the present.

In the vicinity of Whitehorse, Yukon Territory, is a most

unique cemetery. The graves are covered by what appears to be small dollhouses. Placed inside these small enclosures, or close to them, are numerous household items put there by loved ones. The departed are thought to need such things for their life in the world beyond. This practice is very ancient and speaks dramatically of the belief of people in survival. From the civilizations of antiquity to the noise and clamor of the world of the twentieth century this unquenchable belief still prevails.

Indications of Evidence Based on Man's Innate Drives and the Need for Satisfaction

We experience hungers common to all and correspondingly they are satisfied. When there is a craving for food, external reality meets that need, and there is a like response when we are thirsty. The sex drive finds fulfillment as do our desires to create.

Fundamentally, the hunger for perfection and completion is gratified. God has placed eternity in our hearts, and ultimate satisfaction cannot be denied. To realize all of our dreams, to exhaust all of our powers of mind, and to bring to fruition all of our vast creative powers, we must reach beyond our earthly limitations. We realize but a fraction of our abilities and talents in this brief lifetime, and our hunger for further progress and achievement is answered by endless opportunities on the other side.

John S. Bonnell in his book *I Believe in Immortality* quotes Victor Hugo, French poet and novelist, on this inspiring thought: "Winter is on my head, and eternal spring is in my heart. The nearer I approach the end, the plainer I hear around me the immortal symphonies of the worlds which invite me...For half a century I have been writing my thoughts in prose, verse, history, philosophy, drama, romance, tradition, satire, ode, song – I have tried all. But I feel that I have not said the thousandth part of what is in me." (26)

I have not included a summary for this chapter because of the format of the material. It is in itself, with exceptions, a summarization of the 27 areas suggestive of survival.

SOURCE NOTES

1. Crookall, Robert. *The Supreme Adventure*. London: The Camelot Press, 1961, p.10.
2. Barrett, Sir William. *Death-Bed Visions*. London: Psychic Book Club, 1952, p.26.
3. *Chicago Daily News*. Monday, October 18, 1976.
4. The International Association for Near-Death Studies, Inc., Box U-20, The University of Connecticut, Storrs, Connecticut 06268.
5. Rogo, D. Scott. *The Welcoming Silence*. Secaucus, New Jersey: University Books, 1973. p.184.
6. Muldoon, Sylvan, Hereward Carrington. *The Projection of the Astral Body*. Samuel Weiser Inc., 1970. p.316.
7. James, William. *Human Immortality*. New York: Dover Publications, Inc., 1956, p. 319.
8. Muhl, Anita M. *Automatic Writing*. New York: Helix Press, 1963, p. 92.
9. Crookes, William. *Phenomena of Spiritualism*. London: J. Burns, 1874, pp. 109-110.
10. Tyrrell, G. N. M. *Apparitions*. New York: Collier Books, 1963, pp. 35-36.
11. Wickland, Carl A. *30 Years Among the Dead*. Hollywood: Newcastle Publishing Co., 1974, p. 15.
12. Banks, Hal N. *An Introduction to Psychic Studies*. Bend, Oregon: Maverick Publications, 1980, p. 113.
13. Starr, Deane. "The Crying Need for a Believable Theology," *The Humanist*, Vol. 44, Number 4, July-August, 1984, p. 16.
14. Aurelius, Marcus. *Meditations*. New York: Walter J. Black, 1945, p. 99.
15. Tweedale, Charles L. *Man's Survival After Death*. London: Grant Richards, 1925, p. 11.
16. Koestler, Arthur. *Roots of Coincidence*. New York: Random House, 1972, p. 32.
17. Aurelius, *Meditations*, p. 103.
18. Moses, Stainton. *Spirit Teachings*. London: Spiritualist Press, 1962, p. 16.
19. Barclay, William. *Spiritual Autobiography*. Grand Rapids: William B. Eerdmans Publishing Co., 1975, p. 58.
20. Tweedale, *Man's Survival After Death*, p. 11.

21. Barclay, William. *The Apostles' Creed for Everyman*. New York: Harper & Row, 1967, p. 366.
22. Sanford, Agnes. *The Healing Light*. St. Paul: Macalester Park Publishing Co., 1972, p. 72.
23. Fosdick, Harry Emerson. *The Meaning of Prayer*. New York: Association Press, 1942, p. 97.
24. Smith, Leslie R. *From Sunset to Dawn*. Nashville: Abingdon, 1979, p.23.
25. Bauman, Edward W. *The Life and Teaching of Jesus*. Philadelphia: The Westminster Press, 1960, p. 220.
26. Bonnell, John Sutherland. *I Believe in Immortality*. New York: Abingdon Press, 1959, pp. 13-14.

"Everything that exists is in a way the seed of what will be."
— The meditations of
Marcus Aurelius

CHAPTER IV

Our Adventure Following Death

You've reviewed 27 indications of evidence that I feel attest to the continuity of life following physical death. From my personal perspective, it is time to quit playing games and admit that there is enough evidence to say survival is more than an object of pure faith, but is indeed fact. I concur with the late Bishop James A. Pike that it is facts plus faith. This is the proper mix.

Death is the beginning of a new phase of reality, a gigantic step in our growth and development. We've been created in the image of God, have an intrinsic worth and need eternity for the complete realization of our vast potential.

What actually happens when our physical journey is complete? This is what we will now consider in orderly progression and, as we have already seen, there is remarkable consistency of viewpoint and perspective. It is as if a golden thread has been woven through the garment of history delineating each step of our pilgrimage toward eventual perfection.

Death is Painless

In those final moments prior to the transition, there is a powerful, forceful manifestation of the inner human spirit. Dr. Lewis Thomas, noted medical doctor, poet and essayist, speaks of the death experience in this way: "...death may not be the rattling, agonized event that human beings fear. When death is imminent, the brain apparently realizes that pain can no longer be useful as an alarm to spur escape, so the pain is turned off and replaced by a kind of blissful surrender..."[1]

It is in the process of dying that pain is frequently felt, but not in the moments of transition. The ravages of disease or any serious illness are afflictions of the physical body, but in no way do they trouble the spiritual body. The surgeon, William Hunter, when near death, said: "If I had the strength to hold a pen, I would tell how easy and delightful it is to die."[2]

It has been said that death is easier than the birth experience.

Some doctors and nurses have noted that with some patients, when death approaches, there is feeling of radiant joy and exultation. They are between two states of consciousness, drifting out of one into the other. It is similar to dreaming. Our spiritual nature begins to gain ascendency as it prepares to leave its mortal home. Thank God, we are no longer in exile; we are going home to a reality that is impossible to know on this level of consciousness.

Karlis Osis and Erlendur Haraldsson, in their book *At the Hour of Death*, tell of a 69-year-old stroke patient who was partially paralyzed and depressed.

"Suddenly his face lit up, pain gone, smiling—he hadn't been cheerful until then. He said, 'How beautiful,' as if he could see something we couldn't see. And then, 'No body, no world, flowers, light and my Mary (deceased wife).' He was released and peaceful, went into a coma and died shortly after."[3]

Death-bed Visions

Near the time of disengagement of the spiritual body from the physical, it is not unusual for terminal patients to clairvoyantly see friends and loved ones who have predeceased them. These death-bed visions are occasionally confirmed by nurses and physicians, and are not delusions but are objective reality to those who have experienced them. The patients were fully conscious, not in a hypnogogic state, and were not heavily sedated; neither were they hallucinating. They were perfectly aware of where they were and what was going on around them.

A friend of mine, who at that time was a nurse in Anchorage, Alaska, was assigned to care for a terminally ill patient. She reported that the dying person held repeated conversations with his wife who had died three years earlier. The nurse said the man was completely lucid, not sedated, and in full control of his faculties.

Near the end of his physical life, my wife's uncle suddenly raised up in his bed and said, "There's Earl!" Earl was my wife's father who had died previously.

When Dr. Martin Luther King, Sr., preached his last sermon at Ebenezer Baptist Church in July, 1975, he spoke about his deceased wife in this way, "I don't want to make her sad. This is not an occasion for sadness. It is no accident that my wife visited with me sometime between midnight and this morning..."[4]

These discarnate visitors celebrate a joyous reunion with the one who is ready to go home and they serve as an escort committee. You will not be alone when making the transition from death to life.

Robert Crookall, author of the book, *The Supreme Adventure*, tells us that the person who is ready to depart sends "...out a kind of 'call' to friends and relatives who have gone before."[5]

It is a fact of God's marvelous love that the new adventure is truly a homecoming prepared for us by those we love and cherish.

While most terminally ill persons who have had death-bed visions see discarnate loved ones, some have also glimpsed great vistas of magnificent beauty that they will soon enjoy.

Dr. Karlis Osis, in his excellent monograph, *Deathbed Observations by Physicians and Nurses*, tells of a nurse who reported: "A six-year old boy dying of polio described heaven, stating he saw beautiful flowers, heard birds singing, stated he was going to this beautiful land."[6]

Author Matthew Josephson writes of the last hours of Thomas A. Edison: "In the early days of October it became generally known that only a short time was left to him. His mind became befogged at last, his great eyes dimmed, and from time to time he sank into a coma. At the brief intervals when he was conscious he was placed in a chair by one of the tall windows of his bedroom, overlooking a great sweep of lawn and handsome beeches. Could he still see? Mina Edison was the last person he appeared to recognize. She bent over the pale invalid and placed her mouth to his ear so that she could communicate with him. 'Are you suffering?' she asked. 'No, just waiting,' he replied. Once he looked toward the window and the last audible words he uttered were: 'It is very beautiful over there.'"[7]

In those last moments when the powers of the physical body are waning, the spirit is becoming increasingly sensitive, clairvoyant and there is a great expansion of consciousness. The whole psychic stream has been intensely activated in anticipation of the forthcoming journey.

Our Two Bodies

When you stand in front of a mirror you see only one body, your physical. In reality we have two bodies; one is the physical body which you can see; the other is the spiritual body which for the moment you cannot see. In the New Testament, the Apostle Paul is explicit about this. He says, "If there is a natural body, there is also a spiritual body." (I Corinthians 15:44)

The physical and spiritual bodies interpenetrate while we live and function in the earth environment. In the process of death, the physical body dies, freeing the spiritual body which is permanent and enduring. It is the vehicle of expression in the next dimension. It should always be remembered that the physical body is not the authentic you; it is strictly a temporary integument.

Our spiritual body is a true replica, an exact duplicate of our physical body. Arthur Findlay in his masterful book, *On the Edge of the Etheric*, received the following message from the other side through medium John Sloan: "I have a body which is a duplicate of what I had on earth, the same hands, legs and feet, and they move the same as yours do. This etheric body I had on earth interpenetrated the physical body. The etheric body is the real body and an exact duplicate of our earth body. At death we just emerge from our flesh covering and continue our life in the etheric world, functioning by means of the etheric body just as we functioned on earth in the physical body. The etheric body is just as substantial to us now, as the physical body was to us when we lived on earth. We have the same sensations. When we touch an object we can feel it, when we look at something we can see it. Though our bodies are not material, as you understand the word, yet they have form and feature and expression. We move from place to place as you do, but much more quickly than you can."[8]

The spiritual counterpart of our body is perfect; without blemish or disability. Those who have lost a limb in this life need not fear that the spiritual body will mirror this imperfection. It is perfect and whole. It should also be noted that the spiritual body has definite form and, as I have mentioned before, is our vehicle of expression.

The etheric body, as Arthur Findlay defines it, is the seat of our personalities and faculties of mind; our selfhood. We function as whole persons with emotions, feelings and desires. We are complete individuals in every detail. Following the transition we are ready to function in our new environment. These light and airy bodies are as solid as our former earthly bodies that we recently discarded.

Talk about Lincoln's *Emancipation Proclamation*, we've been delivered of our heavy, clumsy and cumbersome physical garment. Liken it to a suit of armor that we've been encased in for many years. We are now rid of it forever. The sluggishness has disappeared and we experience an overwhelming sense of movement, freedom and thought.

This light and perfect spiritual body is such that it can at will pass through solid obstacles; through doors, walls and ceilings. Jesus' body, as the Bible explains, had no difficulty passing through major barriers. In John 20:26, we read that, "A week later his disciples were in the house again, and Thomas was with them. Though the doors were locked, Jesus came and stood among them..." In no way does matter impede the movement of our etheric bodies.

What do we know about the composition of our spiritual body? Communicators who possess such bodies are our prime source of information. We are told they are fashioned quite differently than our previous earth form. We've already mentioned they are exact duplicates of our human organism; solid, tangible and without any disfigurement or defect.

These transition bodies have weight, color and form. They are directed by and are under the supervision of the mind. They respond to a different level of vibrations; much higher and far more rapid than those that directed the activities of our physical bodies.

A variety of terms are used to describe the make-up of our spiritual bodies, but the key word is energy. It is a mental-spiritual energy. Stewart Edward White, in communication with his wife, records her words in *The Betty Book: Excursions into the World of Other Consciousness*. She said that: "I have a definite body and not a vaporous or fuzzy one either. It is a finer-grained substance than flesh. It is not fluid, but mobile. It is more sensitive, more easily acted upon; and at the same time more indestructible, more durable, more self-protecting. You would recognize in it a refinement of matter, a little understood etheric combination..."[9]

The thrill of it all rests in the fact that we are free at last of the encumberances imposed by our temporary residence in the physical body.

The Silver Cord

Coincident with any discussion of our two bodies is the reality of the silver cord. While on the earth plane our physical and spiritual bodies are connected by this cord or energy cable. It can be likened to a telephone or magnetic lifeline. However, when this cord is severed it means the death of the physical body. The spiritual body is then released to continue its pattern of growth and development on the other side.

Just as the umbilical cord has to be cut before we fully achieve entry into this dimension, so it is that the silver cord must likewise be severed before we make our exit from the physical body. On occasion clairvoyants have observed the gradual loosening and complete severing of the silver cord.

During sleep our spiritual bodies separate from the earthly tenement and literally travel the vast reaches of the universe. The silver cord is that flexible and elastic. We are out-of-body when this occurs, but only for a limited period of time. It is only when this silver cord is completely cut that there is a final separation of the two bodies.

There is ample Biblical evidence for the existence of the cord. Open your Bibles to the Old Testament Book of Ecclesiastes, Chapter 12, verses 6 and 7. Here we observe: "Remember him-before the silver cord is severed, or the golden bowl is broken; before the pitcher is shattered at the spring, or the wheel broken at the well, and the dust returns to the ground it came from, and the spirit returns to God who gave it."

In my book *Introduction to Psychic Studies*, I cite a story about Andrew Jackson Davis witnessing the phenomena of seeing the spiritual body leave via the head of his friend. "He tells how he saw the spiritual body withdraw itself from the mortal and issue from the head of the dying person first as a cloud of luminosity that hovered above the bed and was attached by a fine luminous cord – a sort of psychical umbilicus – to the dying person's head. This cloud then slowly took the form of the person, and this form continued to hover over the recumbent mortal body, attached to it by the cord of light just as a captive balloon might be moored to the ground..."[10] As long as any trace of this cord remains, and it does take time for it to dissolve, death does not take place.

IN SUMMARY

Before our summary of this chapter, a cautionary note: all parts of our treatment of survival must be considered in light of the whole. Again, liken it to a jigsaw puzzle. It isn't until the last piece is put securely in place that we get the complete picture. There is an amazing and absolutely fascinating coherency about our examination of the continuing journey. Treat our study as a whole and think in terms of the sum of its parts.

1. Death is painless.
2. Near the moment of transition, death-bed visions of predeceased loved ones are frequently seen. Our rites of passage, with few exceptions, will be with an escort. We do not make the journey alone.
3. Each of us has two bodies, a physical and a spiritual.
4. These two bodies are connected by a lifeline called the silver cord. When this energy conductor is cut, the physical body is discarded. The authentic or real you, the spiritual body, pursues its relentless adventure in another state of consciousness.
5. Death is but a prelude, a continuing journey.
6. View all facets of the paranormal as inseparable parts of the whole. View them only in oneness of theme and substance.

SOURCE NOTES

1. *Time Magazine*, 1979. Vol 113, Number 20, p.87.
2. Hampton, Charles. *The Transition Called Death*. Wheaton, Illinois: Theosophical Publishing House, 1979, p. 22.
3. Osis, Karlis; Haraldsson, Erlendur. *At the Hour of Death*. New York: Avon, 1977, p. 168.
4. *The Anchorage Times*. Anchorage, Alaska, July 28, 1975.
5. Crookall, Robert. *The Supreme Adventure*. London: The Camelot Press, 1961, p. 10.
6. Osis, Karlis. *Deathbed Observations by Physicians and Nurses*. New York: Parapsychology Foundation, 1961, p. 28.
7. Josephson, Matthew. *Edison*. New York: McGraw-Hill, 1959, p.484.
8. Findlay, Arthur. *On the Edge of the Etheric*. London: The Psychic Press, 1931, pp. 142-143.
9. White, Stewart Edward. *The Betty Book*. New York: E. P. Dutton and Co., 1937, p. 66.
10. Banks, Hal N. *Introduction to Psychic Studies*. Bend, Oregon. Maverick Publications, 1980, p. 41.

"And ever near us though unseen,
The dear immortal spirits tread,
For all the boundless universe
Is life — 'there are no dead.'"
— John Luckey McCreery

CHAPTER V

The Moments of Transition

What do you experience in those actual moments of transition when you vacate your physical tenement and step into another room of the Creator's house? We have already seen that pain is non-existent and you are bathed in peace and serenity. Your clairvoyant faculties, acute and sensitive, welcome loved ones who have been summoned to provide light, comfort and support on the pathway to your new adventure. You do not make that transition alone and unaided.

It would seem that near the final separation of the physical body from the spiritual, the one undergoing the experience has a presentiment of what is happening. The mind remains alert despite the weakness and deterioration of the body, although at times it can become lethargic or drowsy. The sensation of floating or rising is frequently experienced. The death bed situation is similar to a halfway house; the spiritual body is slowly departing the physical body.

The denouement, the final moments of bodily imprisonment, have arrived. You have the distinct sensation of floating upward and you find yourself an observer of friends and relatives standing around your inert physical body. The separation has occurred. You make an effort to touch or to say something to your grieving loved ones, but there isn't any response.

In this present condition all physical restrictions have vanished. The room below becomes indistinct; a haze or mistiness makes everything look unreal. It can be likened to flying in an airplane. You look out of the window through floating and fleecy clouds, and only occasionally do you catch glimpses of the landscape below.

Your earthly experience now seems dreamlike as you slowly become aware of your new surroundings. In *Life Beyond Death with Evidence*, author Charles Drayton Thomas speaks with his sister on the other side and she describes her awakening: "It is difficult to realise I have been here so long a time, it seems no more than a few weeks; for there is so much to do, to see, and to learn. I am glad to have known before my passing something about this life and the possibilities of communication with you. Before finally leaving earth I seemed to be dreaming, and yet it was not wholly a dream. It seemed as if I had come here before the final separation from my physical body. I was only partly conscious towards the last, only half within the body; for my soul was already freeing itself. Nor did it seem wholly strange to me when I found myself here. I must have frequently come during sleep; for I could now remember that I had been here previously."[1]

You are home; in a new state of consciousness and ready for new adventures in your ongoing pilgrimage. However, it must be remembered your death experience is uniquely your own. While sharing common characteristics with others who have made the transition, yours can vary in particulars. We have already seen the remarkable consistency of evidence relating to all facets of psychical research, but it is comforting to realize God treats us as unique individuals.

Am I Really Dead?

In the hours immediately following the transition, the newcomer to the world of spirit may not realize that death has occurred. Earth events are still uppermost in the mind and the traveler is still very close to the old familiar environment. He may note indistinctly the death bed scene with the worn-out physical body surrounded by disconsolate loved ones. Any attempt to make contact meets with failure. Relatives can neither hear nor see the departed. The spirit is bewildered and frustrated at the lack of total response.

The new spirit finds himself in his spiritual body, which is indistinguishable from his old physical tenement, and with his consciousness intact. Like an automaton, he aimlessly attempts to go through the motions of some of the things he did in his previous existence.

Then, he meets and recognizes an old friend who had predeceased him and the realization finally sinks in; he, too, has died. This is the great awakening and the new spirit becomes conscious of the change that has so recently been made. Helpful friends, who are not only familiar with the new arrival, but with the present environment, lend their sympathetic and warm assistance. Confusion and bafflement soon give way to understanding and comprehension of what has occurred. We do not face this new experience alone, because it is the nature of things that on the other side guidance and help are always available. It is to be expected that a familiar face or two will be present to give greetings.

How tragic it is that the majority of individuals who pass from one room in God's house to the next make the change completely oblivious to what they will find. No wonder they are so muddled, upset and confused. Those who have spent decades immersed in conservative and fundamentalist theology appear helpless and perplexed. They may express astonishment that Jesus wasn't waiting for them, or that they are in the company of those they knew to be evil or unrepentant on the earth plane. For many believe, after all, that only "good" Christians are eligible for the imperishables of heaven.

How comforting it is to know that the Creator's love and sympathetic concern are evident at every stage of our journey.

Rest – Recuperation – Adjustment

Before the next phase of the journey begins, the newly arrrived individual may need a period of rest and readjustment in order to get "everything together" mentally and emotionally.

The earth environment, in many instances, may have been an exhausting experience. A lengthy illness could have depleted the body's energies and resources. Fatigue or depression may have played havoc with the mind, and severe psychological problems could have been debilitating and disruptive of life.

It is necessary that there be a suitable time for rest and recovery for the one who faces a continuation of life on the other side. The time varies, depending on the particular needs of the immigrant, who has so recently made the transition.

Children and youth, who are physically and mentally sound, may need far less time to adjust to their home or, perhaps, none at all. Communicators on the other side say that the recovery period may be as little as three days; others speak of months or years.

Sudden death, with its attendant panic, confusion and bewilderment, means an indefinite stay in a rest home or hospital. The terrors of war, suicide and accident are reflected in the lives of those whose physical bodies have been so suddenly and tragically extinguished. The shock brought about by the unnatural, premature and sudden severing of the silver cord is so severe that the victim requires extensive reorientation and preparation before he is able to move on. Just as on earth, skilled doctors and nurses, as well as other hospital personnel, minister to all who have recovery needs. Communicators on the other side tell of the fully equipped and sophisticated hospital type environment. It is reassuring to know that our every need will be met when we move from this level of awareness to the next.

The Whole Person Survives Death

While we shed the outer body when we move on, we survive as whole persons. We have seen that our spiritual or etheric body is an exact duplicate of our former physical form. In all phases of our continuing journey the essential components of personhood, body, mind and spirit, are present.

Following the death experience, there isn't any intervening time when we are disembodied, for it is the whole embodied individual that interacts with the environment.

In 1898, William Newton Clarke wrote the following descriptive words: "...If one looks back, death is the end of a career; if forward, it is the beginning of a career; but in reality death is neither end nor beginning, but an event in a career, an experience of life. It closes life in one scene, and opens life in another; but what we often call two lives are but parts of one life of the spirit, which moves on through both unaltered by the change. In this single and continuous life of the human being, death is only a change of scene and conditions."[2]

In speaking of the dissolution of the body, it is incorrect to talk about the immortality of the soul. If we do, it gives the impression that upon the death of the physical apparatus, only the life-giving force continues its existence sans body or form. Greek thought was prevalent in the days of the infant church and the term immortality of the soul was essentially associated with Greek thinkers. In fact, they felt that the body was an irritant to the soul and we best be rid of it.

To be a person means to have a body. There is a wholeness to personality and its expression requires a vehicle. We do not ultimately become disembodied spirits.

What Actually Survives Physical Death

When we discard our physical bodies, what survives?

Priority number one is personal identity; a sense of selfhood. Individuality, with its hierarchy of personal pronouns, indicates that we will continue to be whole persons, and able to recognize our uniqueness and separateness.

Closely associated with personal identity, is the capacity to remember. Any concept of selfhood must include memory. In Hornell Hart's *The Enigma of Survival*, the author points out that "...'my past' is essential to my own sense of identity. When a person loses his memory (as in amnesia) he has to ask: 'Who am I?'"[3]

Memory is not disrupted at the time of the loss of our physical form. It has continuity.

While not all opinion is unanimous, many psychical researchers who have studied the survival question are confident that some or all of the following survive:

1. Selfhood.
2. Memory.
3. Consciousness.
4. Personality.
5. Character.
6. The life principle.
7. The soul.
8. Emotions.
9. Mental characteristics.
10. Intelligence.
11. Perception.
12. Spirit.
13. Creativity.
14. Imagination.
15. Feelings.
16. Faults.
17. Virtues.
18. Habits; good and bad.
19. Skills.

There is obviously overlapping in the above list, but I think it is helpful to have a rich perspective, as complete an overview as possible, as to what survives.

The late medium, Arthur Ford, sums it up rather well in commenting upon survival when he says that personality, complete and integrated, survives bodily death.

IN SUMMARY

1. In the early moments of the transition there is the feeling of drifting, perhaps of floating, and the earth environment becomes less and less real. The final moments of bodily imprisonment are ending.
2. Your new adventure has begun.
3. In the early moments of the transition the newcomer may not realize he has died.
4. Old friends and relatives, with sympathy and understanding, help to clarify the situation. The realization slowly comes and the newcomer begins to make his adjustment to the new state.
5. Too many individuals make the transition without any preparation and an almost total state of bewilderment and confusion are evident.
6. For many making the transition, rest and recuperation are needed before the new adventure really begins.
7. The whole person survives death.
8. Personality identity is paramount.

SOURCE NOTES

1. Thomas, Charles Drayton. *Life Beyond Death with Evidence.* London: W. Collins Sons & C., 1937, p.61.
2. Clarke, William Newton. *An Outline of Christian Theology.* New York: Charles Scribner's Sons, 1898, pp. 449-450.
3. Hart, Hornell. *The Enigma of Survival.* London: Rider & Company, 1959, p. 223.

*"Who can tell but that this
which we call life is really
death, from which what we call
death is an awakening."*
— John Fiske

CHAPTER VI

First Steps

The Receiving Station or Staging Areas

Following the transition, the spirit, having been met and greeted by loved ones, enters a reception center or receiving station. Some refer to it as a vast staging area; others call it "paradise" in referring to Jesus' word to the repentant thief, "I tell you the truth, today you will be with me in paradise." (Luke 23:43)

All the newly dead enter this reception center. The period spent here is dependent upon many factors and cannot be measured in terms of earth time. Individual differences remain the prime consideration when the matter of time is discussed.

In that this is the vestibule or threshold of the spirit world, the newcomer finds that it is almost a replica of the physical environment that he has so recently departed. This lessens the possibility of a severe psychological or environmental shock. He finds himself in a back-home-like atmosphere, and has difficulty believing that he has changed his state of consciousness.

The newcomer's spiritual state, if weakened by repeated transgressions of God's moral law, prevents him from actually witnessing the alluring loveliness and beauty of the environment as it really is. But, while there are limitations, induced by his lack of spiritual sight, he is still pleasantly surprised by his new surroundings. Only further growth and development will help open his eyes to the many delights, refinements and prerogatives of the spirit world.

According to informants on the other side, this staging area is about the second rung on the ladder of the hierarchy of dimensions, or states of consciousness. Here at this rest stop, check point or place of orientation, the spirit undergoes an evaluation of the minuses and pluses of the recent earth experience and receives a report card. And it is also here the guidance counselor maps out a plan of action for our future growth and development. This is all in a context of love and compassion. This receiving station provides insight and perspective for the traveler.

It is also crucial to know that when we make the transition we carry with us our habits, beliefs, prejudices, attitudes, fears, greed, convictions, hopes, dreams and all of our expectations. Our passing does not confer a crown of perfection, nor do we immediately become candidates for sainthood. These attributes of mind remain as part of our baggage when we make the big move. Whatever defects of mind we take with us can only be removed as we learn the truth about ourselves and sincerely wish to mature spiritually.

In every way, then, we are the same persons immediately following death as before, complete with all of our faults as well as our virtues. Our worn-out physical bodies remain behind, but our mental characteristics remain with us and are unchanged. All of our strengths and weaknesses are still manifest.

The Review of Our Earth Life

Immediately prior to or during the time we spend in this receiving station, we face a searching and most thorough self-examination; an exhaustive review of our earth life. Other descriptive terms for this survey and evaluation have included panoramic memory recall, life review and flashback. Communicators tell us that this life review is accomplished with great rapidity, in chronological order and with every detail vividly displayed. Truth, clarity and complete honesty prevail. There is no place to hide.

Finally free of the limitations of matter, it is now our

subconscious mind that predominates. It contains the complete scenario or moving picture of our life's history utterly without deception or camouflage. With total absorption and extremely heightened powers of memory, we literally relive, not only the pleasurable moments of the past, but are emotionally immersed in the painful and unhappy. Our entire emotional self is fully and completely revealed in this detailed transcript.

What is so forcefully experienced are those times we would rather forget, when our behavior so seriously affected the lives of others. We witness our rudeness, thoughtlessness, unkind and extremely harsh treatment of others with shame and remorse. We are able to enter into the feelings of those we have offended and hurt and now, for the first time, we fully realize the extent of that hurt and its sobering consequences. In these moments of assessment and total appraisal, we see ourselves as we actually are. We witness our successes and failures.

This soul-searching review is intended as a learning experience, for self-knowledge is vital. Self analysis looms large, because only as we are witness to our motives and actions, with the accrued results, are we able to chart our future.

No Deception

How would you like to be stripped of all pretense, sham and deception while still in residence in your physical body? This is precisely your situation when you reach the other side. The Gospel of Mark tells it exactly as it is: "...For whatever is hidden is meant to be disclosed, and whatever is concealed is meant to be brought out into the open. If anyone has ears to hear, let him hear." (Mark 4:22)

Your thoughts will be instantly revealed as well as your emotional state. No deception is possible. In your relationship with others, hypocrisy is disclosed for what it is. You will be known for exactly what you are. Your real or essential self is revealed. This is your spiritual self, and it is in this area that you are fundamentally revealed. Do greed, hate, the quest for power and material desires dominate your life? Or have love and selflessness been your guiding light? In any event, your true thoughts, desires and motivating principles will be clearly evident to all on the other side. The point is this – it is impossible for a person on the other side to deceive. The familiar saying holds true, "People will see through you."

Is There a Last Judgment?

The entire creation is grounded upon God's justice, and it is well that we remember those incisive words from Psalm 24, Verse 1, "The earth is the Lord's, and everything in it, the world, and all who live in it..." God is sovereign, a moral order undergirds all things, and ultimately we will be held accountable for our actions, words and deeds. It is imperative that we take responsibility for our conduct now, for, as we shall soon discover, we reap what we sow.

We have been told that, "...In everything, do to others what you would have them do to you..." (Matthew 7:12)

So, "Is there a last judgment?" The answer is "yes" and "no." We can banish from our thoughts the fear of a last judgment in the traditional theological and Biblical sense. But we make a grave error in thinking we escape God's justice.

There is indeed a judgment — but it is *we* who sit in judgment upon ourselves. All judgment is self-judgment. We are judge and jury. Knowing myself, I assure you, that following the review and appraisal of my earth odyssey, I will render a verdict far more critical than any impartial judge.

Call it conscience, or what you will, but deep within man's inner self is a divine element that, as mentioned above, acts as judge and jury.

During that climactic life's review, we do not face a celestial tribunal, only ourselves. We are not excoriated, condemned or judged by a being of light sitting on an imposing throne separating the sheep from the goats.

Surrounded by loving, compassionate guides and counselors, in these moments of self-judgment, the justice that prevails is softened by love, understanding and compassion. All extenuating circumstances are carefully considered.

Charles L. Tweedale, writing in *Man's Survival After Death*, remarks that, "...This judgment is tempered with mercy and with a perfect ability to fully weigh those circumstances which can often justly be urged in extenuation or mitigation, taking into account the motives as well as the degree of wrong accomplished..."[1]

The moments of judgment are always on an individual basis, while spiritual counselors or teachers are available to provide concrete guidance and direction. Our spiritual healing has begun.

Love is the heartbeat of creation, the cement that binds together the disparate factions of our civilization. It is the cohesive element that civilizes and humanizes us, and restores the moral order. Love of God, neighbor and self have more to do with our ultimate destiny than anything else. Judgment rests firmly on the foundation of love.

We Reap What We Sow

Following our life's review and analysis, and always under the sympathetic supervision of our spirit counselors, we gravitate to the state of consciousness proportionate to our spiritual state. The character we have fashioned on the earth dimension is our passport.

Our character is the sum total of our thoughts, words and deeds, and they accrue as we interact with our environment, especially in our relationships with other people. Assess our day to day living; what we say, how we think and act. Thus character is formed following years of conditioning.

What we really are is what we take with us when we make the transition, and our self-appointed place on the other side corresponds exactly with the strengths and weaknesses of our character. Our earth life style determines our place in the spirit world. However, it can be of a temporary nature as we shall see later.

The profligate, the self-indulgent sensualist, will not be on the same level as the selfless individual who has led a good and decent life. Some speak of the Law of Correspondence, which means that whatever our interior condition happens to be, it will correspond with the external. On the outside we mirror the state of our inward being. The rapacious, greedy and completely selfish person will reflect this state in outward appearance. And this Law of Correspondence is also applicable to the environment. It, too, is a reflection of our inner state.

It should be mentioned at this point that we aren't assigned to a particular level or state of consciousness in the spirit world. It is of our own choosing depending entirely on character.

And so it is that when we make the transition our next homeland will be equal to the state of our spiritual development attained while in the physical body. All will be decided by the individual effort put forth here. In the context of our free will, and by the way we live our lives now, we are preparing for our future; those first steps we take beyond the physical body. The only capital we will have will be our spiritual state perfected in having lived according to the Scriptural admonition, "...Love the Lord your God with all your heart and with all your soul and with all your strength and with all your mind; and, love your neighbor as yourself." (Luke 10:27)

This is a highly significant point that needs to be underscored, because this is where it all begins. One must have love and appreciation of self before it is possible to even comprehend love of God and neighbor.

Please Keep in Mind

While each step in our journey would seem to be self-contained as far as explanation is concerned, in reality, there could be some shades of difference in our developing scenario. No part of the process stands alone. We need to be aware of the sum of its parts. The order in which I have placed the various phases of development that we experience on the other side should be kept tentatively in mind, although I am convinced they do occur. The world of spirit operates on its own terms and procedures, complete with awe, mystery and wonder. I would not like to think that everything on the other side is so cut and dried that little would be left to the imagination.

Like Attracts Like

Isn't it true that we feel most comfortable when we are with those who share the same interests, the same likes and dislikes? Such is human nature. It is frequently referred to as the law of attraction, or, as it is informally put, "birds of a feather flock together." This sums it up. I feel at home with some people; with others I do not.

This is the parable of the spirit world. By nature, by affinity, spirits are drawn together to that particular level of consciousness, or sub-level, most appropriate to the kind of persons they are. Evil attracts evil; good attracts good. It is simply a matter of being attuned to those of like condition. In fact, we gravitate naturally to that state corresponding to our characters. It is true that in the world of spirit, the saint does not dwell with the sinner.

When I say "like attracts like," as previously mentioned, I am referring to the fact that each of us goes to that particular place for which, by character, we are uniquely suited. Look at those with whom we frequently associate. We spend time with friends that we enjoy and with whom we feel most relaxed. This is normal and natural. Why should it be any different in spirit? But will we ever be with those with whom we differ, who have completely different tastes and attitudes? Spirit communicators tell us we will on occasion see and meet with those who reside on different levels of consciousness. However, those occurrences are brief and casual. It might be compared to walking along a busy thoroughfare. We pass people going and coming. There is an occasional "good morning" or "good afternoon" but, that is the extent of it. We remain in our groups or families, with those of like interests and character until we depart to higher and more refined dimensions.

Those spirits who have attained a higher degree of spirituality may visit with those on the lower vibrational levels. This is usually done in a missionary capacity, in that some of the more highly developed personalities have freely elected to help those on the lower levels achieve a greater degree of spiritual awareness. It is an axiom in the spirit world that those residing in the lower levels of consciousness cannot move freely to the higher planes.

The question is frequently asked as to whether loved ones, friends and relatives are reunited in spirit.

Yes and no. Yes, if we have reached the same level of spiritual attainment. No, if we have not. However, there can be an occasional, but temporary reunion. It is only when we share the same state or condition that we are together. In any discussion of discipline or chastisement on the other side, it is said that separation from a loved one is exactly what we deserve. We have only ourselves to blame. But, mercifully, such a separation can be temporary if we wish it to be so.

Movement between dimensions depends solely upon one's spiritual condition. There aren't any actual barriers, road signs or traffic signals. States of consciousness or dimensions interpenetrate or shade gradually one into another. Any unescorted attempt to penetrate a higher region results in distinct feelings of unpleasantness and we realize we don't belong there. One's perceptions dim and we soon realize that only growth and development are the keys to the higher regions.

Is There a Hell?

Absolutely not, in the sense that we've been led to believe. We can purge our minds of this abominable and blasphemous caricature. How tragic it is that such a theological concept has so sharply distorted our thinking, plunged us into such despair and dimmed our hope and happiness. This need not be so, and it is precisely at this point that we urgently need to reconstruct our theology and life's philosophy. Psychical research can rekindle our hope and optimism when we contemplate our future destiny. Let me knock in the head immediately some of the silly ideas we have about hell. For instance, that statement in the Apostles' Creed, "Jesus descended into hell," is something with which many of us have difficulty. It is an absurd "tongue in cheek" expression especially when you consider what such an assertion can do to a person's psychological health. I question the necessity of Jesus having gone to such a mythical region in the first place. The poor theology contained in the Apostles' Creed is unbelievable, and my lips are sealed when it is repeated in church.

The Apostles' Creed is the oldest continuously used statement of faith in the Christian church. The origin of the Creed stemmed from the need for a precise summary of what Christians should believe, and it was considered a bulwark against heresy. Candidates for baptism received instruction in the Creed. Only legend makes the claim that it orginated with Jesus' disciples, although a creed quite similar to the Apostles' Creed existed prior to the end of the second century.

Where do you find in the Bible depictions of sulphurous eternal flames, ridiculous devils running around jabbing cringing folk with pointed pitchforks? The source of such horrible misrepresentations can be traced to the theology of the medieval period of history. The art work and literature of that era were filled with frightening images and are expressions of an absurd theology rampant at that time. In viewing Michelangelo's masterwork, *The Last Judgment*, one can't help reacting negatively. God is resplendent on His throne, solemn in mien, separating the sheep and the goats; in this final moment of decision, some are consigned to an everlasting hell and others to eternal ecstasy.

This painting is enough to scare the hell out of anyone. It is all so final. In literature, John Milton's *Paradise Lost* depicts Satan, Beelzebub and Lucifer prattling around with their devilish masquerade. This poetic portrayal of a non-Biblical hell is a ludicrous figment of the author's imagination and should be taken as such. Talk, paint and write convincingly and you color the minds of generations of susceptible and gullible individuals. We must in our thinking banish forever the unreal conceptions of hell that have held captive the minds of sincere human beings for centuries. Frankly, too many of us have held childish conceptions of our ultimate destiny, and it is about time that we sweep out the attics of our minds.

There is no eternal damnation. Hell is not a geographical state, but is a state of mind or being. As William Alger assures us, "...the wicked go where they belong by their own election, from the inherent fitness and preference of their ruling love...The wicked go into hell by the necessary...love of God, not by his indignation; and their retributions are in their own characters, not in their prison house..."[2] Any perversion of God's opportunities merits the inevitable afflictions. This is in keeping with God's love and sense of justice.

Alger goes on to say that, "...the controlling motive of his life, the central and ruling love which constitutes the substance of his being – this decides every man's doom. The view is simple, reasonable, just, necessary."[3]

It must always be remembered that God's justice demands satisfaction, but only within the context of His love, mercy and compassion. W. T. Stead, victim of the Titanic disaster in 1912, said, and with impact, that "punishment without love is not of

God."

Proof of God's fervent love and compassion for his children are found in three magnificent parables in the Gospel of Luke, Chapter 15. They are the parables of the lost sheep, the lost coin and the lost son. All dramatically illustrate the lengths to which God will go to reclaim those who have erred. The eternal God does not condemn even one sinner to an everlasting hell; all humanity will eventually be redeemed. And, God is always ready to forgive. No individual will reside in a type of hell on a permanent basis. He eventually loses his lease and moves on to larger and more attractive quarters.

Emanuel Swedenborg phrased it precisely when he said, "God let people go to hell because they would be miserable anywhere else," but on the other hand we must think of it as a temporary or restricted state. And there is always the opportunity to turn around (repent), to seek forgiveness and to search for new avenues of growth and development.

We do not know the time involved in a particular state of discipline (you can call it hell), but the determining factor is entirely up to the occupant. Recalling what was said previously, we gravitate to our appropriate level in the world of spirit based solely on the essential character or quality of life experienced in our earth pilgrimage.

The lower rungs on the ladder of spiritual development are the hells spoken of in the Bible where there will be "weeping and gnashing of teeth." (Luke 13:28) Each upward step on this stairway of progress and growth represents a much more refined environment, until we reach dimensions of sheer bliss too magnificent and wonderful to describe. Love rules; peace and contentment reign.

We are concerned with the fate of those who have misused their God-given opportunities, who represent all that is ugly in life, all that is vile, sordid, corrupt and debased. What is their state or condition?

Those who have lived totally selfish and completely narrow lives, consumed by greed and immersed in material pleasures, will find themselves in an environment that is somber, washed out, cheerless and drab. Gloom pervades the atmosphere and twilight conditions are in keeping with the inner state of the resident. There are the dark regions, riddled with foul decay and stagnation; horrible beyond suitable description. This is the habitat of the rapist, murderer and debauched person. Only repentance provides a way of escape.

There is a message in the Parable of the Lost Son. The younger of the two sons received his inheritance from his father. He immediately "...set off for a distant country and there squandered his wealth in wild living..." However, there came a time when he had had enough of riotous living and was faced with starvation and other necessary needs. The Scripture tells us that "When he came to his senses..."[4] it hit him that home wasn't so bad after all. This is exactly the situation of those who are in the lower hells. They must come to their senses, and only in this way do they find merciful release from the dungeons of the lower worlds. Consumed by remorse and guilt, repentance is the only prescription that will bring liberation. The contrite and repentant inhabitant, hungry for release, will find his sentence commuted and new vistas of growth and opportunity will open before him.

We create our own heaven and hell. It is purely mental, because thought forms persist and have substance. William Alger, quoted before, tells us, "It is not our outward abode, but our inmost spirit, that makes our experience infernal or heavenly; for, in the last result, it is the occupying spirit that moulds the environment, not the habitation that determines the tenant...."[5]

A thought is the product of the mind, can assume form, and can be as real as anything we can or have experienced. It is true that thinking makes it so. Remember what philosopher Rene Descartes said years ago, "I think, therefore I am."

The Earthbound

Then there are the earthbound spirits; those whose ties or attachments to the physical sphere are so strong that they find it impossible to break away. They are chained to the earth scene and firmly rooted to specific habits and interests. The earthbound are languishing in a state of utter confusion, bewilderment and ignorance.

Robert Crookall writes in the *Supreme Adventure* that, "...The newly-dead man's attention may be earthwards...seeking revenge, preoccupied with the welfare of those 'left behind' or craving physical sensation or he may be affected by undue grief of mortal friends."[6]

The Gospel of Matthew defines the problems of the earthbound in these words: "...For where your treasure is, there your heart will be also..." (Matthew 6:21)

An earthbound entity can emotionally attach itself to a physical presence. This is known as obsession or the invasion of the mind of an individual in order to gratify some selfish purpose. Alcoholics, drug addicts, or those with strong physical cravings, are frequently the target of the earthbound. I would refer you to Dr. Carl Wickland's revealing volume, *30 Years Among the Dead*, for an excellent treatment of this particular problem of the earthbound.

Earthbound spirits may also be responsible for hauntings and a wide range of influences that afflict those in the physical realm.

It is extremely important that we recognize those dispositions of mind and body that spell difficulties for us when we step from our physical form into the world of spirit. Life styles that include the following spell trouble, as would be obvious: selfishness, greed, revenge, cruelty, rebellion against God, depravity, debauchery, theft, spite, meanness, murder, lying, cheating, drunkenness, drug addiction and miserliness.

All this talk about hell, hopefully, has served its purpose in that it unmistakably illustrates the severity of the penalty for disobeying the will of the Creator. God is not mocked, as we have seen, but the question is frequently asked, "Is there really a hell?" Certainly not in the traditional theological and Biblical sense as we have already seen.

However, this question reminds me of Christopher Marlowe's hero-play, *The Tragical History of Dr. Faustus*. The Doctor has a discussion about the life to come with Mephistopheles, who portrays the devil in Faust's myth and to whom Faust has sold his soul. He remarks, "I think hell is a fable." The reply of Mephistopheles is, "Ah, think so still, 'till experience change thy mind!"[7]

We have talked mostly about the down side, but this must never obscure the salient truth that whatever discipline or punishment we incur is redemptive or remedial. Reformation of character is its sole aim. We receive our just desserts and when freely we recant and seek God's forgiveness, the doors of our private hell are opened. Desire for something better is frequently one of the first steps in the redemptive process. Discipline, on the other side, is never unmitigated or limitless. It has a beginning and an end.

We experience cleansing and not perdition. Cleansing, the removal of impurities of character, is essentially what the word purgatory means, and I find this term quite appropriate in the above observations concerning hell.

What one of us is fit at the time of death to merit a large measure of eternal bliss? None is. It is only as we undergo this cleansing, the rites of purification, that we more fully turn from self to God.

IN SUMMARY

1. All newcomers to the spirit world go initially to a receiving center or reception center. Here our passports are validated and carefully checked. An assessment is made of our particular situation, and counseling given in light of our continuing journey.
2. Following a period of rest and recuperation, based on our particular mental, emotional and spiritual needs, the newcomer faces a complete and thorough self-examination. Every detail of our life will be reviewed under the guidance of spirit counselors. We will see ourselves as we really are, free of reprimand and criticism. In this self-evaluation, we are made aware of our successes and failures and the resulting consequences. It is a rich learning experience holding many ramifications for our future in the spirit world.
3. No deception is possible on the other side. We are instantly known for what we are. Our real self is clearly revealed. Hypocrisy is impossible.
4. There isn't any "last judgment" as found in traditional theology superintended by a personage sitting on a great white throne. However, God is a God of justice. All judgment is self-judgment, because deep in man's inner nature is a divine element that acts as judge and jury. God's love, mercy and compassion are everywhere evident in this act of self-judgment, and all extenuating circumstances are taken into consideration in the process of catharsis.

5. Following our life's review and analysis, we gravitate to the state of consciousness proportionate to our character or spiritual condition.
6. Spirits are drawn together by attraction or law of affinity. Like attracts like. This is, of course, in keeping with our natures.
7. We create our own heaven and hell. Mind is the catalyst. Thought forms have substance. As we think, therefore we are. Hell is not a geographical state, but is solely a creation of our inner state or condition. Folks who misappropriate God's gifts find themselves in a hell of their own selection. Discipline that is incurred is only for the purpose of cleansing. The spirit always has opportunity to reform and to advance to a more favorable environment. The door is never closed to the truly repentant.

SOURCE NOTES

1. Tweedale, Charles L. *Man's Survival After Death.* London: Grant Richards, 1925, p. 44.
2. Alger, William R. *History of the Doctrine of a Future Life.* Boston: Roberts Brothers, 1889, p. 434.
3. Ibid., 435.
4. Luke 15:11-32.
5. Alger, William R. *History of the Doctrine of a Future Life.* Boston: Roberts Brothers, 1889, p. 713.
6. Crookall, Robert. *The Supreme Adventure.* London: The Camelot Press, 1961, p. 137.
7. Marlow, Christopher. *Tragical History of Dr. Faustus.* New York: Appleton-Century-Crofts, 1950.

"My own dim life should teach
me this,
That life shall live for
evermore,
Else earth is darkness
at the core,
And dust and ashes all that is."
— Tennyson

Chapter VII

The Whole of the Matter

It is unfortunate that we compartmentalize the world in which we live. We place things in different categories and fail to recognize the creation's unity or grand design. We do not see the whole for the parts, so our vision is faulty. There is a reason for compartmentalization in that it provides a method for conducting the business and work of our society. However, it is imperative that we acknowledge the essential unity and oneness of the created order. Otherwise it makes it extremely difficult to grasp the whole picture of survival. We become so fragmented in our approach to the question, and especially in our thinking, that we fail to grasp the implications of the whole. It is only when we get the overview that we get the big picture. Anything less ends in confusion.

The people of the Far East do not have the problem of separateness. Things are not seen as divided, disjointed or fractional; they are viewed as a whole.

Fritjof Capra, writing in The Tao of Physics, explains that "...The most important characteristic of the Eastern world...is the awareness of the unity and interrelation of all things and events...all things are seen as interdependent and inseparable parts of this cosmic whole..."[1]

Now as a concomitant of this fact of oneness, I would like to put emphasis on this statement: the universe is one.

This is pointed out with finality in conversations with Betty in the book, *The Unobstructed Universe* by Stewart Edward White. She indicates she lives in an unseen but also a seen universe — a whole universe.

Acknowledgment of this fact of oneness is crucial to our present understanding of those states we will one day inhabit. While the entire created order is one, there are different interpenetrating worlds, or states of consciousness, of increasingly finer or rarer substance operating on progressively higher vibrational frequencies.

You might ask, "Where is the next world?" My answer would be, "All around you.' We are talking about worlds within worlds; the interpenetration of spheres or dimensions.

Keep the term vibrations clearly in mind. Think of the first rung on a step ladder as being our own physical existence. Vibrations here are of a low order. We can perceive only within the set frequencies natural to our particular dimension, and our sight, hearing, touch, smell and taste are coordinate to our specific level. The next step on the ladder, following our death, reveals a higher state of vibration; a finer or more rarefied condition.

Communicators reveal that the entire universe vibrates at different rates of speed depending on our particular home. Persons inhabiting the same dimension are attuned to it. They share experiences equal to that level, just as those of us on this physical plane have a commonality of perception and experience.

If you were able to tune to the frequency of a higher dimension, you would interact with those persons who are a step or two ahead of you on the ladder. It is a matter of progression, growth and development.

I believe we can now make sense of what Capra was referring to when he contrasted our sundered view of civilization with the Eastern world view. Unity, oneness, is the key to taking hold of reality. We live in one universe that is completely interrelated and inderpendent.

The Eternal Now

We have seen that by force of habit we insist upon compartmentalizing life; dividing it into manageable segments for purposes of convenience. This also applies when we discuss life after death. We need to remember that there isn't a "before" nor "after." We simply walk from one room in God's house to another. It's as if we open a door, step through, and close it ready to continue our journey. Same house, but different rooms.

Maurice Barbanell, founder of England's *Psychic News*, selects his words wisely in his book *This is Spiritualism*, when he tells us that "...There is only one universe...there is only one life, with an infinite number of manifestations. Each gradation merges into the next. In reality it is wrong to speak of an after-life, or even of a spirit or spiritual world. We are now as much in the spirit world as ever we will be..."[2]

Marcus Aurelius, Roman emperor and stoic philosopher, contributes to Barbanell's convincing thoughts in his *Meditations* when he admonishes us to "Regard the universe often as one living being, having one substance and one soul; and observe how all things act with one movement; and how all things cooperate as the causes of all that exists; observe too the continuous spinning of the thread and the single texture of the web."[3]

When I graduated from elementary school and began my high school career, I was still a part of the same school district. We, then, should not think of eternity as before or after. We should abandon our terribly misleading thought of past, present and future and concentrate on the ETERNAL NOW.

How much easier it is to merely cross over the spiritual bridge from one phase of life, ready for the beginning of the next. There isn't any serious disruption, because life is a continuing journey.

We Are at This Moment in Time
Spirit Beings as Well as Physical Beings

The essential quality of our being is spirit; its essence. It is an indestructible indwelling presence. It is correct to say that we are spirits with a body, and not bodies with a spirit. We live at this moment in eternity and the principle of life is spirit.

The major problem is in seeing life piecemeal rather than as a whole. We conveniently talk of now and then, before and after. This kind of talk creates confusion when referring to the survival question.

The Mind and the Primacy of Thought

The whole of our existence is predicated upon mind. It reigns supreme and stands at the center of our evolution. It is reality. It is the totality of our being.

You do not have a mind; you are mind. To put it in perspective, you can say that mind is the principle of life. In speaking of consciousness, perception, thought, imagination, will, feeling and memory, all are concomitants of the mind.

We should not equate the mind with the brain. The brain is an instrument of the mind, and all expressions of the human body are directed and controlled by the parent mind. When the physical apparatus dies, so does the brain, but the mind is indestructible. It remains the motivating force of the life principle.

Andrew Jackson Davis, writing in *The Great Harmonia*, places the mind in proper perspective when he says: "...I employ the word *mind* in its most extensive application; comprehending the soul, spirit, love, passions, reason and understanding which characterize human beings – all of which terms I use synonymously with *mind*. You will...remember that I am not speaking of any *one* particular faculty or attribute of the soul; but of that entire *combination* of faculties and principles in the spirit of man, which combination I am impressed to term mind."[4]

Life here and on the other side is preeminently controlled by mind, and our thoughts have the power and force of mind behind them to influence the environment; to create and alter substance.

The ability to mold and direct our surroundings is, of course, related to our growth patterns or character in general. The only limitations we experience depend solely upon our spiritual development, or lack of it. One who is accustomed to sordid and irresponsible living, who is completely selfish and only concerned with things of a material nature has little spiritual baggage to bring with him to the world of spirit. He brings little or no appreciation of beauty, love and altruism, so his ability to function as a spirit being is proportionate to his mode of living or life style while on the physical plane until he recognizes the necessity to increase his capacity for a greater appreciation of life's true bounty of love and service to others. Spiritual evolution is the key if the full power of the mind is to be realized, because the only limitations we place on the mind arise directly as a result of our spiritual immaturity.

It is also true that thoughts are things, and that we create solely by the authority of the mind. Many of the limitations that were so restrictive on earth do not exist in spirit. We revel in this newly found freedom. The only limitations we will experience are carried with us and represent the residue of an earth life poorly lived.

In spirit, the full power and play of the mind instantly translates our desires and thoughts into reality. What we conceive mentally we produce, and we create and bring into being those things we most desire. This would include our homes, gardens, clothes, just to name a few of the things we had need of on the earth level.

Emerson put it nicely when he said, "The ancestry of every action is a thought." What we create is in every respect real and solid. There is first the desire, then conception, while form follows.

In like manner the same course is followed while we are residents of the physical body. For example, most of my ministry has been in new church development. While our congregation first met in temporary quarters, a building committee was formed and was given the responsibility of developing plans for a sanctuary and adequate classroom facilities. The committee first brainstormed in an attempt to think through the kind and size building required. Mental activity was the primary step.

Our thoughts were then transferred to paper. The architect responded with the blueprints, and actual construction soon followed.

The equation: desire − application of the mind to the project − conception − birth. This is quite like what we will experience on the other side, only the entire process is profoundly simple.

Mind is the architect as well as builder. We remember that manifestations of the mind, without encumbrances of the physical body, are immediate on the other side. Similar ventures here on the earth dimension are exasperatingly sluggish.

A prime example of the reality of thought on the other side can be illustrated by movement from one place to another. Locomotion is instantaneous. You concentrate on where it is you would like to go, and by thought you are there. However, communicating spirits say that this is a learned experience and takes some doing by the newcomer.

My problem is that I have a grasshopper mind that I have difficulty controlling. If this condition persists when I make the transition, I will have a time of it. I conceive of myself on the other side chatting with an acquaintance and my mind drifts to another locale. I'm gone in an instant leaving a sentence hanging in midair. Hopefully my friend will be sympathetic and understanding. Communication between spirit folk is via thought. Speaking as we do on the earth plane is unnecessary because our thoughts are read instantly. And deceit, deception and hypocrisy are seen immediately for what they are. Because our thoughts will be a complete revelation of our true feelings, some of us may be in serious difficulty on the other side if we fail to clean up our act on this side.

IN SUMMARY

1. The universe is one.
2. Interdependence and interrelatedness are characteristic of all things in the universe.
3. All states of consciousness interpenetrate and are part of the whole.
4. Vibrations or frequencies are qualities of these states of consciousness, ranging from a low order to increasingly finer or higher oscillations as one ascends.
5. The spirit world is not vague or shadowy, but substantial or solid. The lower dimensions resemble our physical world in most essentials.
6. Mind is reality in the world of spirit.
7. Thoughts are things in spirit realms.

SOURCE NOTES

1. Capra, Fritjof. *The Tao of Physics.* New York: Bantam Books, 1977, pp. 116-117.
2. Barbanell, Maurice. *This is Spiritualism.* New York: Award Books, 1967, p. 12.
3. Aurelius, Marcus. *Meditations.* New York: Walter J. Black, 1945, p. 41.
4. Davis, Andrew Jackson. *The Great Harmonia.* New York: Sanborn, Carter and Bazin, Vol. 3, 1856, p. 21.

*"Life is eternal;
and love is immortal;
and death is only a horizon;
and a horizon is nothing save
the limit of our sight."*
  – R. W. Raymond

CHAPTER VIII

Growth in the Ways of Spirit

While age with its infirmities is a problem in the physical state, we'll have no such difficulties on the other side. Free at last of our physical bodies, we revert to the years when we were in the prime of life. We literally think ourselves youthful and we are. What I would consider the prime years may not be so for another. It is strictly our personal decision. Not long following our graduation to spirit, we will wish to match our youthful and vibrant feeling in body with the way we would like to appear to others. Our controlled thinking will make it so. Gone are the deep lines, infirmities and wrinkles of old age because growing old in spirit is not at all equated with the deterioration of our body. We mature, yes, but only as far as wisdom and knowledge are concerned. Our mental faculties are not only ageless but incorruptible.

Children and youth in spirit continue to mature to the age that would be their prime.

What a blessing it will be to remain forever vigorous and youthful in body while at the same time growing in wisdom and stature, and in favor with God and man.

Our physical bodies require constant attention, because eating, drinking and sleeping are required daily routines and dare not be avoided. Geraldine Cummins in her very fascinating book, *The Road to Immortality*, puts it succinctly when she notes, "...On earth men are slaves of the physical body..."[1] The time consumed in keeping our physical body alive and functioning is rigorous and exacting. This is not so in spirit, because this form of slavery has been abolished. What a tremendous reward to be completely free of such impediments, and to be clothed in a body that does not face such relentless daily demands requiring sleep, food and drink, because the environment provides all that is necessary for our bodily maintenance. Communicators tell us that our bodies absorb directly from the atmosphere whatever nourishment we require. However, immediately following our passage to spirit we may still attempt to cling to the strictly mechanical regimen of earth. Only with the expiration of time are we weaned from this blind and automatic response to bodily needs to the less restricting satisfactions of spirit life. Free from demanding physical requirements we now have ample time to pursue more rewarding and gratifying activities, primarily those associated with the mind.

Sex and Marriage on the Other Side

Because of the role sex plays while we are physically mandated, the question inevitably arises, "Is there sex on the other side as we experienced it on the physical plane?"

We are told by those who have already traveled to the higher levels of life that the spiritual highs are so wonderful, moments of sexual ecstacy experienced in the flesh are flat and dull in comparison. In that procreation is non-existent on the other side, sex for that reason is unnecessary.

Is there marriage on the other side? No, not in the sense that we know it while in the physical body. If a married couple here share a genuine bond of love and affection, it is their option if they wish to continue together on the higher planes. Harmony and compatibility are the leading indicators. Also there isn't any need for the traditional family unit on the other side principally for the care and nurture of children, so matrimony isn't necessary.

If a married couple has shared unbearable years of strife and conflict on earth, then that relationship is dissolved in spirit. There is little possibility there will ever again be any contact.

If unhappy in earthly marriage, it might be that a congenial companion might be found in spirit. In fact, in whatever condition you may find yourself in spirit, you will be with those who share your likes and dislikes.

The Ladder of Progression

M. H. Tester, writing in the magazine *Two Worlds*, states that, "...I shall live forever, evolving, improving, reaching ever upwards towards a distillation of spiritual purity and levels of life and consciousness that today I cannot know or even contemplate."[2]

There is a law called progress and it is unyielding. In fact, life is evolutionary, and to move backward, or to retrogress, is completely alien to God's created order. This is the tremendous challenge we will encounter when we make the transition. Of course, we have experienced some measure of growth and development here on the earth dimension. Reality is progression. Evolution of the mind, which encompasses spiritual advancement, is the heart of the matter as far as happiness and enlightenment are concerned. Communicators speak of the evolution of consciousness; of an ever-expanding awareness. Evolution, growth, is one of the supreme laws of the universe.

Eventual union with God, without sacrifice of our individuality, is the goal of the spirit self. One of the major reasons why I so strongly believe in the on-goingness of personality for every human being, is that our God-given potential must fully unfold and be totally and completely realized.

In the book *Spirit Teachings*, given through the hand of Stainton Moses, the thought of fulfillment of personality is given credence: "...There will be a period at which progressive souls will eventually arrive, when progress has brought them to the very dwelling place of the Omnipotent, and that there they will lay aside their former state, and bask in the full light of deity, in contemplation of all the secrets of the universe."[3]

Ultimate union with the Almighty, whom I believe is personal, is the goal toward which all strive, and we ALL will reach that goal. We must realize that following our transition to higher levels, we will still retain our earth-seasoned characters. We do not suddenly become omnipotent and omniscient. In other words, we do not become saints, sages nor all-knowing and completely enlightened. Remember, we will have just attended our graduation ceremonies from kindergarten, not high school and college. Graduate school still beckons and it is where the greatest growth and development will occur.

It is tragic that much traditional theology assumes that upon death our final destination is unalterably fixed. If it is hell, we are told there is no further opportunity for repentance nor reformation. This is false and can be safely abolished from our thinking.

Following our transition, we will all get grades, and there will be those with A's and B's; others will incur much lower marks. However, the joy and the promise is that we will be able to boost those poor grades, perhaps even to A's and B's. And what about a respectable C? Our progress on the other side is guaranteed, but it is always based on our willingness and desire to improve our condition. We hold the key to progress solely in our hands.

Arthur Findlay wisely states in *Where Two Worlds Meet* that: "Progress and mental development are encouraged and every man, woman and child born on earth can progress there and reach to heights which are beyond our imagination. Schools, colleges and universities are provided for that purpose, and all of us, if we wish, will benefit when our time comes, from the intellectual and cultural institutions which are provided for minds, ignorant and learned, simple and wise. In Etheria there is no end to culture, wisdom and knowledge, and it is open to everyone to progress along the road for which each mind is best fitted in that land of wider, happier and more delightful opportunities."[4]

When we make that inevitable move from one room in God's spacious mansion to another, we will not be wallowing in idleness or self-satisfaction; we do not remain sluggards, dawdlers and unemployed dolts. God fobid the image of harps and fleecy clouds. If we expect this, we are in for a big surprise.

There is a challenge to spirit life. It is filled with teeming activity and abundant opportunity. Except for those earth-bound individuals, who are provisionally unenlightened and spiritually blind, the average person becomes aware of the enormous challenge to continue to develop and grow. Once the desire is present, progress is possible. There isn't an iota of coercion or compulsion to advance from the spirit's immediate position. We are totally free agents, and it is only when we say, "I'm ready", that we experience the happiness and light that upward mobility brings.

We are told that such growth and development is gradual, and that one steps ahead as slowly or as quickly as both desire and condition permit. Again, we reach a place where we recognize the necessity to expand our horizons, and to seek to grow and mature.

Earth-bound entities may remain rooted in their lower environments for long periods of time. They are attached to the earth scene by old desires and habits. These are the individuals who will have a tough time of it, and will for years forego the joy and happiness that could be theirs if they genuinely wished to unglue themselves from their miserable situation.

Life in spirit, not unlike earth life, is a school with tremendous opportunities for advancement. Think of your life situation in terms of a continuation school. No sooner do you reach one goal than another beckons in the distance.

It is encouraging to know that a teacher or guide is always available once the student is ready. One day you will join those who are already students of master teachers. What a thrill it will be to sit at the feet of Bach, Chopin, Mozart and Liszt if your special interest is music; or, if art is your first love, how about lengthy conversations and workshops with Manet, Van Gogh, Picasso or Rubens? You scientists and philosophers will also have your opportunity to inhale the rich and heady atmosphere created by the presence of the giants of the centuries in your chosen fields.

With my current interest in theology, I would covet the chance to dialogue with the Apostle Paul, and several of the Apostolic Fathers such as Clement, Ignatius and Polycarp. I would also appreciate an audience with the Greek Father, Origen, and how about lunch with St. Augustine, St. Thomas Aquinas and Martin Luther. Sound impossible? Not entirely.

Great libraries on the other side are filled with the great and worthy literature of the ages and you will have eternity to read them all. You name the book and it will be awaiting you. No need for inter-library-loan there.

Museums and art galleries abound with displays that no repository on earth could possibly match, because so much of what we experience on earth had its inception in the higher spiritual realms.

For those who had little or no opportunity to pursue particular interests or hobbies while dwellers in the physical body, the door is now wide open to do just that. All fields of knowledge, including many you may never have heard of, beckon the seeker and the learner, plus you will have the benefit of superb facilities and highly qualified instructors.

No longer is it necessary to earn a living, to eat and sleep, and to be encumbered with a thousand and one details just to maintain the physical body. Health concerns are no more, and mental and body disabilities no longer interfere with the true thrust of living. Our mental acuity is in peak condition, while fatigue and weariness are no longer encountered. Time has ceased to be a major problem especially in the learning process, and because we now have eternity think of what we'll be able to absorb. Our minds, keen and sharp, are now capable of blotting up knowledge. What a joy. Now, I believe we can finally appreciate the statement that our physical experience represents the kindergarten of the soul. We are taking our very first steps.

The Reverend Charles Tweedale claims, and rightly so, that "...God's purposes to manward are educational and progressive, and have been from the first."[5]

The Apostle Paul sums it up magnificently when he says, "...Now we see but a poor reflection; then we shall see face to face. Now I know in part; then I shall know fully, even as I am fully known." (1 Corinthians 13:12-13).

Do We Work or Are We Unemployed?

We have seen that the other side is filled with activity, both purposeful and leisure. Boredom is unknown. Free of the constant needs associated with the physical body, and now with freedom of choice, you select the occupation you wish to follow, the one that will bring you the greatest happiness, peace and contentment. If, while in the physical dimension, you were happy with your calling, you may wish to continue in spirit, as long as it was one that contributed to the common good. Whatever might be your selection, your natural inclinations, aptitudes and interests would obviously be taken into consideration.

The criterion followed on the other side with respect to your chosen work is directly related to the question of whether it will benefit others and be of service to them. It relates to the joy that one can experience in knowing that you are doing something for others that you will find most stimulating and rewarding.

Should it really be any different here on this plane? We are told in the Bible to love our neighbor and to render service on every level of opportunity.

If your earthside occupation was satisfying and fulfilling, it would be yours to continue on the other side. You will have endless opportunities to sharpen your skills, to work with master craftsmen and to learn new techniques that had previously been unknown to you. Perhaps you're ready for a change and would welcome a chance to do something other than you did prior to receiving the gold watch; to learn a new trade or to enter one of the professions such as law, medicine or theology. The possibilities are endless.

One thing we know – you'll no longer need be concerned with boredom, drudgery or constant routine. Your concern on the other side is not to worry about earning a living, but to do something with purpose and in which self-fulfillment will be a goal. Serving others and providing enlightenment for them is one of the major factors in job selection. It might be that you'll opt for additional schooling or training. Whatever your skills or talents, a wide variety of opportunity awaits you. The arts are especially conspicuous and distinguished on the other side. A career in art or music may be appealing and, although you may lack specific training, you will have unlimited and unbounded occasions to learn. Whether it be science, engineering, medicine, law, theology, philosophy, the crafts, music, gardening, you have but to name it, and the door will open. It would be impossible to totally catalog or name the occupations that are available on the other side.

But, what if you should tire of what you are doing? Provision is made in the event this should happen. Freely, you make the switch to something with a greater challenge and occasion for happiness.

Leisure time activities are also paramount, although work can serve as a form of recreation for many.

The diversions of culture are always available, such as plays, concerts, museums and art galleries. The sports minded will not suffer for lack of something to do, and those who wish to continue to massage the mind, why not a visit to the vast spirit libraries? A myriad of events, pleasures and other fun activities are readily available. The environment of the etheric world is entirely conducive to the joys associated with the out-of-doors.

In support of this, turn to Anthony Borgia's book *Life in the World Unseen*, where you will read, "And it must be remembered that indoors or outdoors are precisely one to us here. We have no changes of weather during recurrent seasons. The great central sun is forever shining; it is never anything but delightfully warm. We never feel the necessity for a brisk walk to set our blood circulating the better. Our homes and houses are not necessities, but additions to an already enjoyable life. You will find many people here who do not possess a home; they do not want one, they will tell you, for the sun is perpetually shining and the temperature is perpetually warm. They are never ill, or hungry, or in want of any kind, and the whole beautiful realm is theirs to wander in."[6]

Just as progress on the other side of the physical order is limitless, so are the opportunities for advancement and mental enlightenment. Communicators inform us that it is impossible to put into words the joys to which we have to look forward.

IN SUMMARY

1. By the process of thinking it is so, we remain forever young – in our prime. Children and youth grow and mature until they reach the age where they look and feel the most comfortable.
2. Our spirit bodies, without infirmities or blemish, do not require food or drink. We are no longer slaves to the physical body.
3. Sex as we now know it in the physical envelope, is unknown on the other side.
4. Marriage as we now know it is also unknown on the other side. If a genuine bond of love and affection existed on the earth dimension, it can and possibly will, continue on the other side. Love is the cement. Those who were mated unhappily on the earth plane, will not be together in spirit, but it is entirely possible that a mate will be found in the spirit realms.
5. Growth and development never cease on the other side. It is a law of the universe.
6. Ultimate union or communion with the living God is the common goal of all in spirit.
7. The spirit dimensions teem with life and activity. Boredom

is unknown.
8. All useful occupations exist in spirit. We can continue our earthside work or we have the option of selecting another. The choice is ours.
9. Leisure time activities abound with a menu of culture, continuing education and sports.

SOURCE NOTES

1. Cummins, Geraldine. *The Road to Immortality.* London: Ivor Nicholson & Watson, 1933, p.45.
2. Tester, M. H. *Earth is Education's Kindergarten.* Two Worlds. August, 1973, p. 208.
3. Moses, Stainton. *Spirit Teachings.* London: The Spiritualist Press, 1962, p. 16.
4. Findlay, Arthur. *Where Two Worlds Meet.* London: The Psychic Press, 1951, p. 68.
5. Tweedale, Charles L. *Man's Survival after Death.* London: Grant Richards, 1925, p. 39.
6. Borgia, Anthony. *Life in the World Unseen.* London: Psychic Press, 1969, pp. 141-142.

"This world is not conclusion;
A sequel stands beyond,
Invisible, as music,
But positive, as sound..."
— Emily Dickinson

CHAPTER IX

Everyday Life on the Other Side

Imagine what it would be like to spend a day on the other side?
You have already seen that life on the other side consists of different levels all commensurate with the degrees of spirituality you have attained. If you sluffed off your earthly responsibilities and disregarded God's plan designed especially for you, then you have some work to do.
This point is succinctly expressed in a small book called *Sunrise*, published by the White Eagle Publishing Trust in England. White Eagle, speaking from the other side, tells us that "...A man who has lived only to worship mammon or riches will find himself very poor afterwards, in very poverty-stricken surroundings. Having little spiritual substance in himself the man has little with which to build his home. His environment will be a replica of his inner self, himself externalized."[1]
Your environment is self-created and is based solely upon the degree of spirituality you have carefully nurtured while functioning in your earth circumstances. This will make an enormous difference in what your life will be like following the transition.
Suppose that your earth life, like so many others, was average as far as deportment was concerned, neither spiritually brilliant nor despicably tarnished and sordid. You are sort of middle-of-the-road. You have just stepped through the gate of death into

the vestibule or lobby through which all newcomers must pass. You have already read that this may lead to a brief or indefinite stay in a hospital or rest home, and either, or very soon, you will thoroughly review your earth pilgrimage. The preliminaries completed, you then go to your self-appointed place.

Now you are ready for your adventure in living. You will find yourself on that particular level of consciousness precisely equal to the growth patterns you have already achieved. It is a perfect match. Your associates are also matched to your tastes and interests. Your environment has form and body. Your spirit body is also an exact duplicate of your earthly appearance.

In that you did not squander your earth opportunities in riotous and debauched living, you now are able to reap what you have sowed. You note your surroundings are infinitely more beautiful and colorful than anything you ever observed and treasured on earth. Your eye marvels at the vivid and unbelievably appealing and awe-inspiring countryside and you find that it is quite similar to what you had previously enjoyed.

You joyously perceive:

lovely landscapes	gardens
towering mountains	trees
hills	orchards
rolling plains	grasses
lakes	flowers
seas	animals
groves and woods	fish
forests	birds
valleys	

You immediately feel very much at home, but what you are experiencing is beyond description, ineffable. How could you possibly describe these incredibly magnificent surroundings to an earthling?

By now you revel in the freedom of your spiritual body. Earth limitations have disappeared. Your senses are acutely alert and unrestricted. Your consciousness is vastly expanded and your level of awareness is amazingly enlarged. Your finer and lighter body is capable of instant locomotion, and movement from one place to another no longer depends upon automobiles, trains, buses and airplanes. You travel on the wings of thought.

Awaiting your interest and discovery are:

1. Occupations favorable to your taste, talent and creative endowment.
2. Recreation appealing to every desire and interest.
3. Well stocked libraries.
4. Fascinating and intriguing museums.
5. Art galleries.
6. Colleges, schools and universities.
7. Vast sports facilities.
8. Motion pictures and theaters.
9. Every type of cultural activity imaginable.
10. Seminaries; a variety of theological institutions.
11. Academies of Art.
12. Places of worship.
13. Laboratories.
14. Clubs and social organizations catering to all interests.

All that you have known and loved in this present mode of expression is found on the other side. There is more than adequate provision for all who are sincere in their desire to mature.

You will also find cities, towns and villages which are magnificent in design and constructed with materials unexcelled in quality and beauty. Your place of residence in the spirit domain will be as you want it to be. If you were content with your earthly habitation, you might wish a replica in the spirit. Here the power of the spirit is the creative agent and with its twin, desire, the home of your dreams becomes a reality. Your home in spirit, whether lavish or modest, complete with furnishings, will tell much about you and where you are on the ladder of progression.

Reliable communicators tell us that:

1. Spirits noting they are naked following the transition are instantly clothed through the power of visualization, an adjunct of the mind. Clothes also mirror the person's inner spiritual qualities or lack of them. The higher the development, the more exquisite and beautiful the raiment. (Spirits who have mastered the intricacies of mental activity associated with channeling, and who are seen clairvoyantly, are usually wearing clothes familiar to friends and relatives.)
2. Grime, dust, dirt or, for that matter, any unsightliness, are

absent in the spirit realms.

3. Nature's disasters are entirely absent; no earthquakes, floods, tornadoes, hailstorms, windstorms, smog, or any other inconveniences that interfere with daily life on the other side.

4. Permanence and not decay or deterioration are hallmarks of the spirit world. Although change can be brought about through the medium of the mind, the new arrival is conscious of permanence, stability and durability. What a drastic change from the impermanence, decay and corruption of our former earth habitat. Note the permanence of the individual. There is no death. Note the permanence of your health. There is no sickness nor disability. Note the permanence of your place of residence. There will be no changes unless you so desire.

5. There is no need to make a living in spirit for the purpose of paying your bills. You are forever free of this earthly necessity. Your only duties are those that are self-imposed. However, the selflessness you seek to attain comes from service to others and the involvement in some type of useful activity. There is a necessary balance between service and those things which enrich your personal life.

You'll be delighted to learn that money is an unknown in the spirit world, because there isn't anything to buy. The riches of the kingdom are yours to enjoy without counting the cost. Enjoy the theater, concerts, sports events and a myriad of other activities without having to purchase tickets. All institutions of higher learning, featuring a multitude of subjects dwarfing anything known on the earth plane, await your interest and without any consideration of tuition.

6. You have already seen that in spirit there isn't any need to eat and sleep. Your etheric or spiritual body does not require nutrients or sustenance. There is an inexhaustible life force that quickly supplies or revitalizes any depletion of energy your fine, highly-tuned body may need. Thus, sleep isn't necessary because that life force is a constant source of replenishment.

You slaves of the kitchen will have no further worries concerning meal preparation, clean-up and worries about staying on a diet.

With the elimination of sleep from your schedules, and the escape from the kitchen, think of the additional time you'll have to concentrate on the real essentials of living.

7. Darkness in the spirit world is non-existent. Anthony

Borgia, citing remarks from his communicator, notes "...It is perpetual day. The great celestial sun forever shines...Here we have no recurrent seasons of spring, autumn and winter. Instead we enjoy the glory of perpetual summer — and we never tire of it!"[2] However, with the vast power of your mind, it is entirely possible to bring into being any condition pertinent to that particular season which is your favorite. I enjoy a touch of the seasons. Endless sun would, for me, become a bit monotonous.

You'll not have to worry about checking that thermostat hanging on the wall. With the even and constant warmth provided by the continual sunlight, the temperature discomforts and disagreeable weather conditions endured on the earth dimension are entirely absent in spirit. In fact, shelter isn't needed, because the spirit does not have to tolerate extremes of heat or cold.

8. Conversation in the world of spirit need not be as we know it in the physical apparatus, but is the product of telepathy. However, some communicators say that when a spirit wishes to engage in an earth-type conversation, it is entirely possible, but not necessary. Conversation is via thought and is instantly understood by the other person.

9. Time and space as we experience them as earthlings, may, as the philosopher Immanuel Kant has said, be "forms of perception' in the world of spirit. We can only experience and report on them subjectively. The philosopher and scientist can only speculate. However, speculation is not only permissable but necessary.

I am a slave of the clock and time to my way of thinking is strictly linear or sequential. We live in the A.M. or P.M. We measure all of our activities by watching the face of the timepiece. This is not true concerning the other dimensions or states of consciousness.

Beyond our physical existence, it is possible that the past, present and future exist simultaneously. Speak of the ETERNAL NOW. On the other hand, time may not at all be a factor in spirit, nor need we be overly concerned with its passage. Permanence, an eternal existence, affirms that time is inexhaustible on the spirit planes. The best part of it, then, is that we are ageless, so the passage of time is inconsequential. In speaking of time, "...For a thousand years in your sight are like a day that has just gone by, or like a watch in the night..." (Psalm 90:4).

Space and time, according to physicist Albert Einstein, are to be seen as a whole. In consideration of space, we have read that the various dimensions interpenetrate and are not to be viewed as separate domains. Spirit folk do not have earthly spatial limitations and can penetrate barriers without a problem. Space exists then from one point to another.

IN SUMMARY

1. How well you enjoy everyday life on the other side is dependent upon the level of your spirituality following your transition.
2. You will feel at home in your new environment, because it will have some similarities to your earth experience.
3. Your new surroundings will far surpass anything with which you were familiar in your previous habitat. But remember your environment will be a mirror reflection of your level of maturity.
4. Your spiritual body will be far less subject to the limitations you were so well acquainted with in the physical body. Your consciousness will be immeasurably expanded. Your freedom will be exhilirating.
5. What you have known, enjoyed and loved on the physical plane are found in spirit. However, words cannot possibly describe how superior they are.
6. In the non-physical world mind is predominant. It is the creative agent. Thoughts are things, literally.
7. By visualization, mental effort, you create your own personal wardrobe.
8. You will live in a tidy world on the other side. Pollution, grime, dirt, decay, deterioration and natural disasters are all absent in the spirit world. Permanence and not decomposition is the norm. There isn't any such thing as wear and tear.
9. There is nothing of the 8 to 5 work routine, because money is not a medium of exchange. No income tax nor monthly bills to worry about. You are rich without measure, and you can enjoy a galaxy of activity without cost.
10. You will have no need for food or sleep. The life force keeps

your energy level high.
11. An even and comfortable warmth pervades your environment while perpetual sunlight is yours to enjoy.
12. Communication, conversation, is by telepathy.
13. Time-space are unlike the earth dimension. We can speak of the eternal now in that past, present and future may exist simultaneously.

SOURCE NOTES

1. Eagle, White. *Sunrise*. Liss, Hampshire, England: The White Eagle Publishing Trust, 1958, pp. 28-29.
2. Borgia, Anthony. *Life in the World Unseen*. London: Psychic Press, 1969, p. 31.

"...This is rather an embryo state,
a preparation for living. A man
is not completely born until he
is dead."
— Benjamin Franklin

CHAPTER X

Preparation for our Journey in Spirit

This is the most important chapter in the book. Read it carefully, for the suggestions found here will save you much anguish and bewilderment when you begin your new adventure on the other side.

Awareness is the key. If we know the nature of the future state, what we might expect, we can prepare ourselves accordingly on this level of life. We have seen how our destiny depends upon today's decisions. Poet John Oxenham's words speak for themselves:

> "To every man there openeth
> A way, and Ways and a Way.
> And the High Soul climbs the High Way,
> And the Low Soul gropes the Low.
> And in between, on the misty flats,
> The rest drift to and fro.
> But to every man there openeth
> A High Way and a Low.
> And every man decideth
> The Way His Soul Shall go."[1]

I recently read that Christians face death with more fear and trepidation than adherents of any other religion. How tragic and unnecessary, for a thorough understanding of death, and what we might expect following the transition, can markedly reduce any apprehension and anxieties we may have.

Frequently I think of Bishop James Pike's statement that it is faith plus facts that provide the mix of our confidence. We continually seek to build on a firm foundation of faith, buttressed by facts given by those who are resident in the higher dimensions, and who are so eager to communicate the good news about life beyond.

Those of us in the lower grades of spiritual and mental development have much to learn in order to eliminate the ignorance and superstition that blind us to the actual conditions on the other side. We are frequently reminded that it is the quality, the character of life here and now, that determines our spiritual status in the realms beyond.

Emanuel Swedenborg proclaims in his book, *Divine Providence*, that "...In the spiritual world, into which everyone comes after death, the question is not asked what your belief has been or your doctrine, but what your life has been. Was it such and such...?"[2] How ample are our spiritual and mental assets? We cuddle our material possessions like the golden calf and give little or no thought to our personal growth and development. What will we actually take with us when we depart for another shore? Certainly not our personal material property or belongings. One's social status will mean absolutely nothing nor will vanity.

If God and things of the spirit remain as an afterthought as we struggle in our physical environment, this will severely diminish our capacity to both appreciate and enjoy the new life that will one day be ours. It will be as if our eyes are closed, our feelings dulled and our minds hobbled by our insensitivity to a different level of spiritual awareness. A vast program of re-education will be necessary or more valuable time will be lost in our progress to higher states of consciousness.

We have already learned that many who pass from this plane to the next reach their destination in a state of confusion. They haven't experienced a spiritual awakening, and their new level of reality is like a dream world, unrecognizable and bewildering. Their surroundings are at variance with what they have previously known, and they are totally unprepared for what they have found. The most seriously perplexed and confused are the rigidly orthodox, those who are unyielding and inflexible in their beliefs. Only through re-education over a very long period of time will their eyes be opened.

When we speak of this life being a preparation for the next, we need to take advantage of every opportunity to develop our spiritual natures. All God asks of us is that we do the best we can and allow him to do the rest. How reassuring this is, for it simply means that we are not battling alone against the forces that put a curb on our efforts to attain spiritual maturity.

One word continually stands forth as the sum and substance of our search for maturity, and that is LOVE. It encompasses the whole of our effort to merit the indescribable and sublime joys of the higher states of consciousness. William T. Stead (1849-1912) gives beautiful expression to the heart of the matter in his book *After Death*:

> "Love is God, God is love. The more you love, the more you are like God. It is only when we deeply, truly love, we find our true selves, or that we see the divine in the person loved...Love is the fulfilling of the law, love is the seeing of the face of God...If you wish to be with God—Love! If you wish to be in heaven—love...! Love! Love! Love! That is the first word and the last word..."[3]

So in all our efforts our intent is to water and cultivate the seed of love until it blossoms and spreads through every facet of our personality. In Thomas Merton's *Seven Story Mountain*, he lets us know that simplicity, wholeness and love are what constitute good lives. How simple it is for a writer and teacher to admonish others, especially when suggesting standards of conduct. There is a certain glibness that too often creates anxiety in those who sincerely seek to love but who measure growth in terms of a snail's pace.

I freely admit, with embarrassment, that I do not measure up to what I have said about the preeminence of love. My poor attempts to love God and neighbor are still miniscule and feeble. However, let us all take heart because life is a struggle for each of us. It is only with God's help that we are able to achieve any semblance of progress, and even then it is painfully and agonizingly sluggish. We do manage to plod on, and recall that the most august of saints speak of the dark night of the soul.

We will, no matter how large our efforts to love, even at the point of physical death, be only on the threshold of that effort and capacity.

Seeking Help

We need first to recognize that God hears our cries for help as long as we, even though feebly, put our trust and faith in Him. Our efforts may be weak, but He acknowledges even the slightest progress on the spiritual path. I'm always greatly heartened when I hear the words: "Ask and it will be given to you; seek, and you will find; knock and the door will be opened to you. For every one who asks receives, and he who seeks finds, and to him who knocks it will be opened." (Matthew 7:7-8) In our search it is extremely important to keep in mind that God does answer prayers.

In the suggestions that follow, you might say, "Yes, but how will I ever be able to heed your recommendations?"

First, be sincere as you seek God's help and guidance. Believe that He answers your prayers. The Holy Spirit, God in action, will speak to your need, rest assured. In Psalm 25, a lament as well as a petition, the psalmist recognizes God as teacher, and with great expectancy, utters these words:

> "...Show me your ways, O Lord,
> teach me your paths;
> guide me in your truth and
> teach me...
> Good and upright is the Lord;
> therefore he instructs sinners in his ways.
> He guides the humble in what
> is right and teaches them his
> way.
> All the ways of the Lord are
> loving and faithful
> for those who keep the demands of covenant..."
> (Psalm 25:4-5; 8-10).

Seek with optimism and expectancy and rest assured that the wise and compassionate God will direct your ways and will give you light upon your path.

It is always comforting to know that we are never very far from the influence and wisdom of our guardian angels or spiritual guides. In seeking spiritual fulfillment, these ministering spirits are eager to help provide those "holy nudges," inspiration and personal guidance needed to help us upon our way. Each of us has a guide, or perhaps several, who are shepherds from our birth through the moments of physical death. Guardian angels make every attempt to influence us telepathically.

We do not pray to our guides, but to God, asking him to help us make contact with those who are committed to our care and spiritual oversight. They cannot help us unless we acknowledge they exist and are anxious to assist us. We then must be completely receptive to their creative influence.

It isn't the purpose of a guide to take over the direction of our life. We remain captains of our own souls and responsible for our actions. We need, however, to be aware of and to take advantage of the free and unfettered minds of those who, with missionary zeal, reach out to each of us. They can provide some light to illuminate the many dark areas that restrict our growth.

Guardian angels or guides may be loved ones or personalities we have never known, but who have literally adopted us. They are frequently very much like ourselves in temperament, personality traits and abilities. They are familiar with our habits, our personal needs and what is best for us. It is tragic that so few people acknowledge the presence of their spiritual teachers, because they are so eager to contact us and to provide comfort and support. In preparing, especially, for that great adventure that awaits us all, our guardian angels await our call for assistance. Speak normally and naturally to them, not in the attitude of prayer, but in a conversational tone. Get acquainted and your life will be infinitely better for it.

Some Suggestions to Help in Your Search For Spiritual And Mental Maturity

1. Acknowledge that God is preeminent in your life.
2. Seek to develop a capacity to love yourself, God and your neighbor.
3. Always continue your search to better understand yourself, because this is the road to psychological maturity.
4. Develop a meaningful philosophy of life and death.
5. Develop an optimistic and positive outlook on life.
6. Dispel negative attitudes.
7. Develop self-control.
8. Cultivate a sense of joy in your life.
9. Be humble.
10. Be patient.
11. Strive to be a person of integrity.
12. Tell yourself that you can make changes in your life. Believe it.
13. Accept responsibility in all areas of your life, especially for your actions.
14. Seek always to be realistic about life.
15. Constantly cultivate an open mind. This is extremely important.
16. Develop the capacity to forgive.
17. Develop a capacity to learn from your mistakes without becoming discouraged.

The Apostle Paul told us it is imperative to grow up and act like adults. There shouldn't be any doubts that the password for our project preparation is maturity. He further sympathetically urges us to forget what is behind and strain toward what is ahead, pressing on to our goal.

A number of years ago, while rummaging through a stack of books in a thrift store, I found an ancient copy of E. Stanley Jone's *Is the Kingdom of God Realism?* In his provocative volume, Jones points out "...That there are four outstanding things that disrupt the human personality and with it human society; resentments, anxieties, selfishness and a sense of guilt..."[4]

The self-centered are the self-disrupted. In our reach toward maturity, I would nominate the word self-centered as the most descriptive adjective that is interpretative of the human dilemma. Selfishness is a massive stumbling block and it severely retards our progress toward our spiritual goal.

The master plan for each life rests upon a two-tiered foundation: God, who provides the means by which we can have the power, expertise and knowledge in order to achieve our goals; and ourselves, by using our individual reason and creative abilities given us by the Supreme Director of our lives.

It is well to remember that the Author and Finisher of our faith will never let us go until we achieve a dramatic union with him. For this Psalm 100 gives some expression of how we ought to feel:

"Shout for joy to the Lord, all the earth.
Serve the Lord with gladness;
Come before him with joyful songs.
Know that the Lord is God.
It is he who made us, and we are his;
We are his people, the sheep of his pasture.
Enter his gates with thanksgiving and his courts with praise;
Give thanks to him and praise his name.
For the Lord is good and his love endures forever;
His faithfulness continues through all generations."

Ways to Foster Our Growth and Development

1. Regular attendance at the church of your choice.

I sincerely believe that the church, warts and all, is a community of seekers dedicated to the awakening of our spiritual senses. I do not intend to abandon the church because my theology differs, sometimes radically, from mainstream theological and Biblical perspectives. God alone is Lord of the conscience. However, locating a church that encourages you to chart your own personal theological course is extremely difficult to find. That I recognize.

Fellowship is the heart of the church, while in matters of belief it must be left to the individual to confirm only those things that feel absolutely right to him. For, as Leslie D. Weatherhead uncompromisingly states, truth is self-authenticating. The service of worship gives us regular opportunity to praise and thank God and to seek strengthening in our preparation for life on the other side.

Hopefully your church considers education so vital and important, especially for adults, that it has assumed the character of a mini-theological seminary. An indispensable relationship to the whole would be a first-class library. It is unfortunate that most churches think of a library as an afterthought in their building plans.

The church, always attempting to reform itself, should without fail recognize the interface between religion and psychic phenomena. The "signs and wonders," so evident in the early Christian church, are woefully lacking in the majority of today's churches. Supernormal phenomena undergirded the life and work of the infant church and, for that matter, such phenomena is clearly evident in the world's living religions.

It is psychic manifestations that give religion its vitality, energy and spirit. Unfortunately, we have substituted creeds, tradition, doctrine and dogma for those life-changing signs and wonders so clearly evident in the Bible. Abundantly visible are instances of healing, clairvoyance, clairaudience, precognition, materialization, telepathy, altered states of consciousness, psychokinesis, the miracles and gifts of the Spirit. We need only read the Book of Acts to get the message.

In our pursuit of a consistent and compelling understanding of the death experience, we dare not avoid the psychic dimension that clearly permeates all religions.

We can note with joy and thanksgiving that more denominations are open to consideration of paranormal phenomena.

An example of this increased openness to at least examine the subject is found in the United Presbyterian Church in the U.S.A. (Now the Presbyterian Church, U.S.A.). In 1976, the Church's General Assembly, the governing body of this denomination, approved a *"Report on Occult and Psychic Activities"* which was made available to individuals, pastors and congregations. It offered guidelines for those who are confronted with occult and psychic questions and problems.

It was a monumental and highly significant report, nonjudgmental and fair. It contained an outstanding bibliography and definition of terms. The report, it should be emphasized, was only intended to provide specific guidelines "...in dealing with these matters..."[5]

It is too bad that the more conservative and fundamentalist

churches, those with a closed system of theological and Biblical thought, are the least likely to welcome the open-minded and, especially those who consider psychic phenomena integral to spiritual growth.

However viewed, regular church attendance is a plus in your personal preparation for your journey beyond the gates of death.

2. A systematic and disciplined study of Scripture.

This is another imperative in your preparation. Your church should provide a wealth of opportunities to help you find your way through the Scriptures. I would also recommend that you use one of the modern translations of the Bible, such as the *Revised Standard Version, Today's English Version, The New International Version, The Jerusalem Bible, the New American Standard Bible*. A paraphrased version, such as the *Living Bible*, is not recommended. A disciplined daily approach to Bible study will pay rich dividends in your quest for direction and inner peace.

I would also commend to your reading and understanding the Scriptures of the world's living religions, such as Hinduism, Buddhism, Islam and Judaism.

When the Scriptures are approached prayerfully and expectantly, God indeed will reveal His will for our lives. Remember that specific plan for your life. To find your path through the thickets of bewilderment and confusion, it is necessary to continually seek His guidance, knowledge and wisdom. I am convinced that in some marvelous way, God as Spirit, is unambiguously revealed and we receive light upon our path. We need never despair.

3. Practicing the Ancient Art of Meditation.

Prayer involves conversation with God, while in meditation you listen. Both play a definitive role in your preparation for spiritual maturity and your ultimate adventure. Each serves a different function, but there is an obvious kinship.

Meditation is a discipline whereby you go deep within while concentrating on a single object, mantra, word or phrase. It is the mind that plays the prime role as you seek integration of self and a deepened relationship with God.

For those who persevere there are rich rewards. The results achieved can be inner peace, relaxation, alleviation from stress greatly renewed energy, pronounced physical stamina and alertness of mind. One cannot minimize the tremendous effort and discipline needed to reap the great rewards that are evident in the lives of those who are willing to pay the price.

Book stores always have on their shelves material concerning meditation. The reading approach to the ancient art can be productive, but enrollment in a class also has its merits. With people of like mind and interest, the group effort might be the most rewarding, because you'll have strong support to continue your undertaking and not become discouraged.

4. A study of the classics of psychical research.

Remember that religion and the paranormal interface. They are twins and dare not be separated. Each gives energy and vitality to the other. All of the world's living religions are heavily impacted with psychic manifestations. It is essential that you be knowledgeable in this area of concern.

There is an abundance of titles under the subject. The bibliography at the end of this book is evidence of that. While an author is occasionally reluctant to recommend a book he has written, I am not. *Introduction to Psychic Studies* will provide you with an excellent overview of the paranormal as well as the spiritual implications. I have frequently cited that crucial to any understanding of what your future may bring, recognition of the link between religion and psychic phenomena is necessary. My book acknowledges this linkage and honors it.

5. A disciplined and regular time for prayer.

To deepen our relationship with God through prayer should be our highest aspiration. Prayer should be a perfectly natural emphasis in our lives, a disciplined exercise that can reveal an unveiling of God's master plan for each of us.

The words found in Jeremiah 29:12-13 are sustaining and reassuring: "Then you will call upon me and come and pray to me, and I will listen to you. You will seek me and find me when you seek me with all your heart..." We can believe these words as we sometimes shudder in the midst of our inadequacies, disappointments and defeats.

Prayer is simply talking to God, while casting aside all stilted jargon and theological double-talk. Make prayer a regular daily habit. Prayer and Bible reading go together, so work out your plan and schedule for both. But, above all, be consistent and faithful in this most rewarding and pleasant task.

I would also recommend that you live for a few minutes each day in the pages of one or more of the time-honored devotional classics. They abound. Their revealing thoughts and inspiration help you move from the noise and clutter of the world to moments of peace, calm and serenity. For starters, I would suggest such classics as *The Imitation of Christ*, *The Practice of the Presence of God*, *A Testament of Devotion*, and any of the inspiring writings of Thomas Merton.

Just what must you believe as you tread your way through the labyrinths of creeds, doctrine and dogma? I've come to the point in my life where my beliefs are few and simple. I have removed the barnacles and encrustations around what I personally feel is the core of the Christian faith. My fundamentals are three: love of self, love of God and love of neighbor – a holy trinity.

Dr. Leslie D. Weatherhead in a Foreword to Raynor C. Johnson's fine book *Religious Outlook for Modern Man*, talks candidly when he says, "The older I get, the more I feel that the essential ideas of Christianity are exceedingly few in number. Of these essentials I grow more and more certain. But their number grows less and less. Around that area of the certain there is for me a vast hinterland concerning which the assertion of certainty seems childish and silly..."[6]

Only you can determine what you believe at this moment in your life. With personal growth it will change, but the freedom of the individual to chart his or her own theological position must be inviolate. In your continuing quest, I make earnest appeal that you put down on paper a personal statement of faith at this point in your life. Periodically this document would need to be amended as your faith grows. In accepting this challenge, you will be leaving the halls of static theological thought, but the rewards will include freedom from the shackles of useless dogma.

IN SUMMARY

1. It is imperative that we know what to expect following the dissolution of our physical body.
2. Knowledge concerning the death experience and the future states will eliminate any fear we may now have regarding our destiny.
3. Material possessions and social status mean nothing on the other side. It is character that counts.
4. Love is the measure of all things.
5. We all fall short of the glory of God.
6. How do we heed the many recommendations to shape up? First, seek God's help and guidance.
7. Our guides or guardian angels are always ready to assist us in any way they are able.
8. Resentments, anxieties, selfishness and a sense of guilt are terribly disruptive in our lives and cause a multitude of difficulties.
9. God and man are partners in the struggle to achieve.
10. Five excellent ways to foster our growth and development are: regular church attendance, a systematic and disciplined study of the Scriptures, a disciplined life of prayer, practice of meditation and a study of the best literature available in psychical research.
11. The essentials of our belief system can be simple and very few in number. Luke 10:27 and Micah 6:8 are suggestive.
12. Prepare a brief statement of what you currently believe.
13. Do not be discouraged in your pilgrimage. Even though we all stumble, fall and backslide God never fails to respond to our pleas for help.

SOURCE NOTES

1. Oxenham, John, *Bees in Amber*.
2. Swedenborg, Emanuel. *Divine Providence*. New York: Swedenborg Foundation, 1970, 1970, p. 73.
3. Stead, William T. *After Death*. London: Psychic Book Club, 1952, p. 14.
4. Jones, E. Stanley. *Is the Kingdom of God Realism?* New York: Abingdon-Cokesbury Press, 1940, p.128.

5. *Report on Occult and Psychic Activities.* The United Presbyterian Church in the U. S. A.. Office of the General Assembly. Prepared by the Advisory Council on Discipleship and Worship. New York: 1976.
6. Johnson, Raynor C. *A Religious Outlook for Modern Man.* London: Hodder and Stoughton, 1963, p.8.

"Love runs into the arms of death and finds not destruction, but the beauty and mercy of life."
— Hugh l'A Fusset

CHAPTER XI

Shalom

Bernard Thompson was a lawyer who loved the sea. He was an avid windsurfer and a common sight at any event that was held by the ocean. He tragically drowned one day while windsurfing. His friends and acquaintances felt he had died purposefully because he was soon to have a foot amputated, was a diabetic and had recently been released from the hospital.

It was suggested that rather than waste away in the hospital, he preferred to die in the ocean that he loved. One day Bernard was reported missing at sunset, and the next day his body was recovered near Barking Sands.

The memorial service that Bernard Thompson's friends arranged was inspirational. It was attended by 400 people from all over the Island of Kauai. The participants gathered at the sand bar between Poipu and Waiohai Beach. All brought flowers or a homemade lei. Bernard's Hula Halau (Hula School) was there and members performed the hulas that he loved.

Following the hulas, the group assembled near two canoes which were covered with leis. Bernard's relatives and friends talked about him as if he were part of the group and listening. His brother spoke about how Bernard had graduated and moved to another level of life. After all had spoken, paddlers got into their canoes that were filled with flowers and his ashes, and moved out beyond the point where they were scattered. A helicopter flew over and dropped flowers on the crowd and water.

Everyone left the memorial service feeling a sense of completion and happiness, knowing that Bernard had enjoyed the moving tribute as much as his friends.[1]

This service pinpointed a remarkable contrast to the usual funeral service. The latter underscores death rather than life, is frequently sterile, solemnly ritualized, and far too long. The beautiful spontaneity of the Hawaiian memorial service can be totally lacking in the usual funeral service.

The canned words used by too many officiants at funerals are stilted and offer little solace or comfort despite the sincerity with which they are spoken. Words intended to comfort frequently invoke fear. It is also an extremely unfortunate characteristic of too many funeral services that the officiant takes for granted that the deceased is a committed person spiritually. Certainly you always give the benefit of the doubt, but, for the soul who hasn't yet made that leap of faith, how can you conceivably share such passages of Scripture as these: "Blessed are the dead who die in the Lord," or "Jesus said, 'I am the Resurrection and the life; he that believeth in me, though he were dead, yet shall he live.'"

There must be a readiness for spiritual commitment and salvation, in the Christian sense, but such a turn-about may not occur on this side of the grave but on the other side. We must be realistic, circumspect and completely honest when saying goodbye to departing loved ones. Let God be the judge of the character of a person's soul.

Faults, weaknesses and especially strengths can be openly faced and discussed, within reason, during moments of bereavement and especially in the memorial service. But, what should be openly stressed is the fact that it takes eternity to fully realize that particular plan God has for the life of the one who has so recently entered another room in God's house.

The following incident occurred in a funeral service in Anchorage, Alaska. A woman's husband had died suddenly and she was understandably distraught. He was something of a bounder, certainly not a church-goer, but who lived by the Scriptural imperative "Love your neighbor as yourself."

The fundamentalist clergyman who conducted the funeral service, made quick reference to the fact that the man had not embraced the Christian faith. He left no doubt in the minds of those present that the departed had now become a permanent resident of hell. The widow, horrified beyond measure, instantly arose and abruptly left the service. What this judgmental minister said was totally thoughtless and unforgivable.

A satire on funerals was one of the creations of Artist-in-residence Mark Packer at the Roswell, New Mexico, Museum and Art Center. His eye-catching exhibit was approximately 10x12 feet and depicted a church sanctuary. Those sitting in the pews were onions, and the casket contained an onion. The officiating clergyman was also an onion.

At each of the four corners of the "sanctuary" there were pillars, and on top of each was a box of tissues. The entire display was electronically rigged, and when the current was turned on, the onion in the casket rose as if being transported with wings to "heaven." Then the air became filled with the odor of onions, and this is when the tissues were meant to be used.

Most persons viewing this exhibit reacted with shock, disdain, contempt, outright anger and, others, with laughter. The artist had skillfully and humorously depicted our traditional funeral services.

A Different and Realistic Approach

Far too many funeral services are dismal. The somber and hushed atmosphere belies the fact that such a service should, in reality, be a celebration of the on-goingness of life. There can be joy amid dignity and reverence. Grief needs to be undergirded by assurance and positive faith in what the future will really bring for ALL who continue beyond the portal of death. The hymns, prayers and eulogy need to reflect an emphatic aura of hope and confidence. These necessary elements are all too frequently missing from the usual tired and shopworn funeral service. Let the officiant say, "Death is Resurrection for the saint as well as the sinner. Death is a release from earthly limitations to a life filled with new opportunities for commitment, growth and development."

Those of us who are confirmed universalists, who definitely believe that God's love is large enough to "save" all mankind, can speak with strong conviction about the fact of personality survival. There isn't anything nebulous about it. And, why not an equal definiteness concerning God's eternal promises? These vibrant promises aren't just a matter of faith. They are fact.

When we dispose of the physical garments, let us do so with

assurance, love and dignity.

The one whom we honor in the service is now free of that heavy outer material husk, is alive and well in the lighter, more free, spiritual body. We celebrate life, not death. We look ahead and not behind except for happy memories. We close one door and open another. With the certainty we have of the continuation of selfhood, this is a plea to say goodbye to the material presence, and to rejoice in the sure and certain knowledge that the one whom we love and remember now has new worlds to conquer.

The Memorial Service

A memorial service held in the home, church or place loved by the one who has made the transition, is much more in accord with a celebration of life.

To promptly abandon the word funeral would also be another step toward neutralizing the pictures and images suggested by the expression. It connotes death, the presence of a corpse, hymns with certain phrases that are archaic and other unrealistic thoughts. It also places emphasis upon the finality of life. It creates an atmosphere, a mood, that is anything but reassuring and positive. To have a separate room for close friends and relatives during the service, and the awkward custom of filing past the open casket, are artificial. We need to help lift the mind to a level strongly suggestive of life and away from the trappings of death.

In my many years of ministry my relationship with funeral directors has always been positive. They are, with very few exceptions, deeply concerned with the welfare of those who seek their counsel and advice. They are moral and decent individuals. They have always welcomed my suggestions and in most cases supported my philosophy regarding the conduct of the service.

A memorial service allows participants to be natural and free of restrictive ritual. In that the body of the departed isn't present, it is so much easier to accept the fact that the loved one has made a good transition, and has gone on to a new and greatly expanded life.

Why not informally and spontaneously share remembered

moments of fellowship and significant experiences that you had with the departed? If friends and relatives are hesitant to speak individually, anecdotes can be given to the officiant who can then share them with those present.

Photographs of memorable occasions may also be displayed. An informal gathering in a memorial service permits tears, hugs and immediate words of sympathy. Serving refreshments can also promote informality and foster closeness. People will tend to linger and share intimate moments with the family.

Another "farewell" in the Hawaiian Islands again illustrates both informality and innovation in a memorial service.

This beautiful service was held on the Island of Kauai at Waiohai/Poipu beach on the lawn of Nukomoi (the old home now owned by the hotel that fronts the beach). It was a service for an artist who was fondly known as Lulu. She was a lady in her 70's, who had drowned while snorkeling off the beach in front of Waiohai. Lulu's favorite chair had been placed on the lawn and was used as an altar. It was surrounded by photos, mementos and special nick nacks that she loved.

The memorial service was conducted by the local museum director, and all of Lulu's friends attended. Following a brief introduction, all the members of the arts community, who chose to speak, related a brief story or anecdote about some interesting thing that Lulu had done.

A special anecdote concerned hot air balloons. She had recently completed a whole series of paintings featuring balloons. So, at the end of the memorial service, everyone inflated a balloon with helium, releasing them while tossing leis into the surf. It was a wonderful going-away party for a lady who enjoyed life and liked to have fun – a true and fitting memorial.[2]

Does Cremation Pose a Problem?

A question frequently asked at the time of transition concerns cremation. Is it advisable in view of what we currently know about the release of the spiritual body from the physical counterpart?

It takes approximately three days for the duplicate body to completely withdraw from the physical. So, it is recommended that in the event of cremation, this time frame be honored. However, nothing can ultimately prevent the etheric body from embarking on its intended journey. With God, nothing is impossible. We are always in loving hands from the birth experience through eternity. No one need be particularly worried about the three-day waiting period but it would be better to observe it if possible.

My instructions concerning the disposition of my remains clearly indicate that I am to be cremated, and the three-day waiting period be observed. However, the time between death and cremation usually exceeds the three days.

One major advantage of cremation is that the body is out of sight, and this eliminates frequent visits to a particular grave site. Prolonged mourning and too frequent graveside visits can hinder the growth and development of the departed one. Extended grief tends to hold the spirit near to the earth plane.

A memorial service followed by cremation underscores what we have already noted, that death is a preface to even greater fulfillment and achievement in spirit. Regardless of whether a loved one is cremated or placed in a gravesite, the spirit finds release, unlimited freedom and unparalled opportunity for spiritual maturation.

IN SUMMARY

1. Many funeral services are completely unrealistic, filled with theological jargon and of little comfort to the bereaved, and are far too long.
2. Many funeral services that are intended to comfort instead provoke fear and discomfort.
3. Officiants at funeral services can be judgmental in tone.
4. Let the clergy speak of God's unfailing love for all who pass through the portals of death. He should mention that all survive the demise of the physical body and will one day completely fulfill God's requirements for that particular life plan.
5. A memorial service, following cremation, is recommended.

A Suggested Memorial Service

A memorial service, usually held in a funeral home or preferably a church, is conducted without the presence of the one being honored. However, tradition should not preclude holding a service outdoors or wherever it would be appropriate, as for example, the two Hawaiian memorial services. Take into consideration the life style, personality and circumstances of the departed.

Anyone can conduct a memorial service or a traditional funeral service for that matter. Whatever your choice, the service should be very personal and not dry, uninspiring ritual.

The service I am suggesting has spiritual overtones but it is entirely possible that you will wish the service to be strictly secular and completely without any religious reference. The dominant emphasis should be, of course, on life, not death, and the continuity of consciousness and change of condition.

A suggested title is *A Memorial Service of Thanksgiving and Witness to the Resurrection* with the person's name, date of birth and date of transition. The parts of the service can include:

Organ Prelude

Call to Worship: The eternal God is your refuge and underneath are the everlasting arms.
Hymn: "The Day of Resurrection."
Prayer of Invocation: Eternal Spirit, in whom we live and move and have our being, in whom our life is your joy, and death only an incident in the eternal adventure to which you call us; bring light out of the darkness, hope out of our sorrow, and comfort that rises out of an awareness of your presence. AMEN.
Scripture: John 14:1-3: "Do not let your hearts be troubled. Trust in God; trust also in me. In my Father's house are many rooms; if it were not so, I would have told you. I am going there to prepare a place for you. And if I go and prepare a place for you, I will come back and take you to be with me that you also may be where I am. You know the way to the place where I am going."
Anthem
Scripture: Psalm 23:
"The Lord is my shepherd, I shall not be in want.

He makes me lie down in green pastures,
He leads me beside quiet waters,
He restores my soul.
He guides me in paths of righteousness for his name's sake.
Even though I walk through the
valley of the shadow of death,
I will fear no evil,
for you are with me;
your rod and your staff,
they comfort me.
You prepare a table before me
in the presence of my enemies.
You anoint my head with oil;
my cup overflows.
Surely goodness and love will
follow me
all the days of my life,
and I will dwell in the house of the Lord forever."
Hymn: "O God, Our Help in Ages Past"
Scripture: Ecclesiastes 12:6-7:
"Remember him-before the silver cord is severed,
or the golden bowl is broken;
before the pitcher is shattered
at the spring,
or the wheel broken at the well,
and the dust returns to the
ground it came from."
Message of Remembrance and Hope:

Some thoughts for you to incorporate into whatever is said about the one being honored:

Death is not the end but the beginning for each of us.

Death is a transition to a new state of consciousness.

We are here to celebrate life not death.

It is natural to die and it is just as natural to survive.

(*Name of departed one*) is clothed in his or her spiritual body and has moved from this kindergarten to a larger school of spiritual reality.

We are told that the best is yet to be. This limited physical existence is but a foretaste of a multitude of wonders we have yet to experience.

We have only just begun to live.

Remember that God has a plan for each life and he assures us that nothing can prevent its completion.

The true self will persist on the other side of death. Character and mental habits survive. Personal identity is assured.

God is the God of the living and not of the dead.

Pastoral Prayer and Lord's Prayer:

"Eternal God, we thank you for the life of _____ _____, and we would remember her/him in this hour of both sorrow and joy. How very grateful we are that life continues beyond physical death, and that_____, in her/his spiritual body, will continue to grow and mature in another dimension of your Kingdom. And, above all, we thank you for the bonds of love that cannot be severed and that reunion with those who have gone before is sure and certain. We also thank you for giving us this hope and promise. And now as we have been taught we humbly pray *The Lord's Prayer*:

> "Our father, who art in heaven,
> hallowed be thy name,
> thy kingdom come, thy will be done,
> on earth as it is in heaven.
> Give us this day our daily bread
> and forgive us our debts as we
> forgive our debtors;
> and lead us not into temptation but
> deliver us from evil,
> for thine is the kingdom, the power
> and the glory, forever. AMEN.

Hymn: "Now Thank We All Our God"
Benediction: And now may you leave this place in the sure and certain knowledge that God loves you and that you will never be separated from him. AMEN.

Organ Postlude

Note: Other passages of Scripture that are entirely appropriate for a memorial service are: Psalm 16; Psalm 46; Psalm 121; Psalm 139; Isaiah 40:28-31; Matthew 22:31-32; Matthew 11:28-30; I Corinthians 15; II Corinthians 5:1-20.

This memorial service is appropriate for most occasions but you will want one that is uniquely your own. Circumstances will determine the components of your service.

Eileen and I recently lost a very dear friend. While Bill was widely known in our area, his wife decided not to have a memorial service. Instead, she set a time in her home when friends were invited to visit. Refreshments were served. In this informal situation comfort and healing were everywhere evident. This was just as effective as a more formal memorial service would have been, and it was exactly what Bill would have wanted. There isn't any set pattern. The important thing is to do what is most comforting to those remaining here, taking into consideration wishes and personality of the departed one.

Rapidly gaining favor in memorial services is a brief reception immediately following the rite. A note in the service bulletin, if there is one, or a word from the officiant, would say, "You are invited to a brief reception following the memorial service."

At a recent memorial service there was a tape of the departed one singing "Open the Gates of the Temple." She had been a renowned singer and it was a most appropriate way to remember her.

If you plan your own memorial service, why not do a tape while in the physical body to be played at that service? It would make the continuing journey more memorable.

SOURCE NOTES

1. Davis, Carol Ann. Kauai, Hawaii. Used by permission.
2. Ibid.

*"I will instruct you and teach
you in the way you should go;
I will counsel you and watch
over you."*
— Psalm 32:8

CHAPTER XII

Questions I've Been Asked

When children die, what happens to them on the other side?

Growth continues in spirit where they are loved, nurtured and cherished. They are tenderly cared for in special facilities by teachers gifted in child care and teaching the young. Frequently these instructors are relatives or close friends who are also in spirit.

Will there eventually be a reunion of parents with their little ones who predeceased them? Yes. However, it may take time. Parents whose lives have made them candidates for the lower dimensions will experience some delay in achieving such a reunion. Recognition of the need for growth, coupled with a strong desire to escape their less favorable living conditions will ultimately bring about a happy reunion.

Will parents recognize their child in that the separation may have been a lengthy one? Through the power of the mind, the child is able to make recognition possible at the time of reunion.

Whenever any death occurs there is only a physical separation. Even though the etheric body of the spirit is invisible, the adhesive of love conquers all separation. Your loved one is closer than before because of the incredible powers of the mind. Psychics with the gift of clairvoyance frequently see spirit entities.

Should we pray for those who have predeceased us?

The answer is a resounding yes. The poet Tennyson has said, "Far off thou art, but ever nigh; I have thee still, and I rejoice; I prosper, circled with thy voice; I shall not lose thee tho' I die." We need to surround our spirit loved ones with our prayers and love. It is natural to still have their best interests at heart and to pray for their spiritual progress. I am convinced that the departed hear our supplications, and we can imagine the comfort and solace they bring, especially following the transition. We need to let them know of our continuing love and warm concern.

Do we see Jesus Christ immediately following the transition?

Any person asked this question must necessarily hedge a bit. All we can do is to indulge in conjecture and surmise. Some communicators have revealed an encounter with a Christ-like being, very similar to the "being of light" mentioned by some who have had near-death experiences. It is my personal opinion that such an encounter with the Christ is reserved for those who are resident in the upper echelons of the spiritual realms. I would not, for one minute, doubt such a meeting but this is probably reserved for the saints.

Much depends on the level of spiritual maturity. It is entirely possible that spirits might "feel" the presence of highly evolved entities who themselves share some of the characteristics of Jesus Christ. And, while not actually seeing Him, it would be enough to be affected and impressed by Him.

I have previously mentioned that, through the passage of eons of time on the other side, and dependent upon our maturation, we will stand in the presence of God. No one dare speculate on such an encounter. We will be in such an exalted spiritual state that description is totally impossible.

So why will it not be the same with the Person of Jesus Christ? In the meantime this high thought should give us sufficient motivation to fashion our lives increasingly in His image.

Isn't it possible to be so overly concerned with the life to come, that we neglect our responsibilities in this life?

Yes, it can be a problem. I've discovered a few individuals so immersed in things to come that they neglected their everyday responsibilities here.

The word "now" is important to what we will experience in the future and we, at our peril, neglect our daily round of duties and responsibilities here. This is our proving ground, our kindergarten, the base designed for the development of our characters. How trustworthy, faithful and dependable have we been in helping society resolve the many problems that afflict each of us, such as war, racism, delinquency and poverty? Are we responsible citizens, and how productive have we been on the job? Have we given "full measure" for the salaries we've received? Have we been ethically and morally honest in our relationships with others? Now is the time to take stock of our lives and to note the pluses and minuses.

With the bulk of our effort centered on the earth dimension, we nevertheless need to be acutely aware of the importance of preparation for the step beyond our present stage of action. Our "centering" on today's responsibilities prepares us for tomorrow.

Theologian John Hick sums up the above thoughts in this way, "We should...accept our mortality as something that God has ordained in His wise love and so live that like the best humanists we can say: 'I do not at present *mind* whether there is an after-life or not; I do not need one to make this life acceptable, for it is acceptable already in its own right'..." (1)

Does marriage exist on the other side?

Not as we know it. However, if two people are happy the union can continue on the other side. This presumes that they are both residents of the same dimension. But, take heart, for sooner or later the couple will be together.

If they are unhappy here, there is little possibility they will ever see each other again. It is entirely likely that a suitable partner will be found in spirit. Love and harmony are necessary for any union if it is to be fruitful and permanent, especially on the other side. I believe that ultimately a perfect union will be achieved on the other side if desired.

Does the devil really exist?

No. While we continue to wrestle with the problem of evil, the Devil with a capital "D" is strictly the product of an over-active imagination. To give evil a human guise and personality, and to refer to "him" (the devil) is neither speaking factually nor realistically. To talk about the devil (small "d"), and as a symbol of evil, has some merit but only for the sake of being descriptive.

The composite figure of a devil, an adversary of God, is taken from sources other than the Christian Scriptures. Myth and legend figure prominently in the portraiture. It was only natural in a primitive and pre-scientific age to place blame for evil upon a manufactured scapegoat. We can delete permanently from our thoughts the fact that the devil is a distinct personality.

Good and evil do exist, and the human animal has a predisposition to make the wrong choices. Evil spirits, undeveloped folk on the other side, do exist and can also play havoc. Malevolent entities, probably earthbound, are very real. It is possible that some mentally ill persons may be the victim of the influence of evil spirits. Our predisposition to subvert the good may also, in some instances, be attributable to malicious entities. However we view the problem of evil we acknowledge its reality and must fight it with every resource at our command.

Do you feel that life after death is still an open question?

Not in the least. It is my personal opinion that the proof is abundantly evident, and obtainable, to the person with an open mind. Hard scientific proof is another matter, but the discovery of truth is never the sole prerogative of the scientist. I am certain, however, that one day we will have scientific proof of the survival of consciousness.

It is an unspeakable tragedy that a closed system of theological thought has prevented us from acknowledging the truth of the statement, "There is no death." What a difference it would make in the lives of millions who are bound by the fear of death and the frightening shadows of a fictional hell.

Why must preachers be so vague when they speak of life after death?

If they are completely convinced of survival, there is nothing of shadow and vagueness in their proclamation of the fact.

Easter morning is the clergyman's most significant opportunity to triumphantly proclaim, "Where, o death, is your victory? Where, o death, is your sting?" (I Corinthians 15:55) There isn't anything nebulous about this statement and the preacher who speaks with this conviction is true to the Gospel and is telling it like it is.

Do people of faiths other than Christian survive?

Absolutely. Survival is part of God's natural order. Death is but the seed and Resurrection the fruit. God's love heralds the fact that not one soul is lost, and each individual will fully realize his or her full potential beyond death.

The religion or dogma one professes plays no role in survival of personality. While faithfulness to one's beliefs, and adequate preparation for one's destiny, are crucial to the quality of life each person will find on the other side, neither reflect on the fact that survival is assured for ALL of God's children.

This should also answer the often asked question about what happens to people who have never heard of Jesus Christ.

Will my pets survive death?

Yes. The bond of love obviously unites a pet and owner, and we are aware that love is stronger than death. This isn't to say that all animals survive, such as chickens, cows, mice and your favorite mosquito. No, only loved pets, and they will be with their owners on the other side. There have been many cases where clairvoyants have seen spirit pets. I can't possibly imagine being on the other side without pets because they add to the fullness of life.

Is it true, as I have been told, that all psychic phenomena is demonic and a thing of the devil?

This is a falsehood propagated primarily by conservatives and fundamentalists who champion a completely closed system of theological thought. Their literal approach to the Scriptures precludes any free inquiry into things of a paranormal nature. They are captive to tradition and espouse a rigid dogmatism in matters of theology. With this mind-set and attitude, is it any wonder they condemn psychic phenomena as demonic and a tool of the devil?

While fundamentalists acknowledge that there is such a thing as unexplained phenomena, and a supernormal element in creation, they refer to spiritual warfare involving demons and the devil. All psychic manifestations, according to the fundamentalists, are the result of evil spirits attempting to thwart the good intentions and purposes of mankind. It is baffling to me how the fundamentalists can explain away the psychic element found in Scripture. It is the psychic components that give the Bible life and meaning and they are crucial to any understanding of the Biblical narrative.

Good and evil are evident in many phases of our life and those passages in the Old Testament, especially in the Books of Deuteronomy and Leviticus, refer to the shadowy side of the psychic stream, often referred to as the occult.

There is a fine line of difference between the occult and genuine psychic phenomena. The term occult means "hidden," or "secret," and concerns such things as witchcraft, magic, palmistry, numerology, astrology, tarot cards and fortune telling, but these subjects are worthy of study. However, one should never confuse these things with the psychic phenomena of telepathy, clairvoyance, clairaudience, precognition and psychokinesis, to name a few.

It is precisely the things of an occultish nature that give rise to the terms demonic and satanic, and to mistaken statements concerning the existence of a devil.

What about those who have committed suicide?

The condition of suicide is not a pleasant one. This act of self murder has cut short a life given by God.

The person who commits suicide is earthbound, and will remain so until remorse and guilt are expunged and he recognizes the imperative need to move higher on the dimensional ladder. Only then will he have the opportunity to move out of his dreary condition. The suicide only postpones what would have been his normal growth and development on each side of the portal. He is the loser. His troubles follow him to the other side. Escape from life's disappointments and problems is impossible. We are told it is far easier to master our emotional problems on this side than the other.

It is reported those who commit suicide appear to be in a mental fog on the other side. They do not at first realize they have died, but eventually they must come to grips with themselves before they find release from their prison houses of the soul. It is often true that those who have taken their own lives deeply regret it. This is the first step toward rehabilitation. This will ultimately happen no matter how many years are spent in earthbound captivity. Hope should never be extinguished, because there is always opportunity for progress no matter how bleak the present may appear. Pray for the release of those who have committed suicide so they may face up to their problems. One day they will see the light and literally move in the direction of their freedom and out of the darkness.

Is it necessary to contact mediums (sensitives)?

There is no great need to have a sitting with a medium. In fact, for some, it is to be discouraged because they have a tendency to order their lives by what they are told.

However, an occasional sitting is all right if the sensitive is a person of integrity and substance. A few years ago, I had a sitting aboard a cruise ship. The cost was modest but the results were not particularly enlightening. Not all sittings are, but as a psychic researcher, teacher and writer, I gained a few insights.

Very few sittings provide evidential or veridical material and most have been disappointing. Prolonged grief over the loss of a loved one can be one of the few exceptions for seeking a sitting. While never guaranteed, an attempt to contact a departed loved one can prove fruitful. The sensitive would need to have high qualifications and be recommended by one who is knowledgeable regarding mediumship.

I would strongly recommend the development of your own psychic capacities, and only consult a sensitive if you thought it absolutely necessary.

IN SUMMARY

1. Children who make the transition are loved, nurtured and cherished. They grow to maturity under the skilled leadership of special teachers.
2. We can and should pray for those who have predeceased us.
3. Depending upon our level of spiritual awareness, it is entirely possible that we will ultimately encounter entities who are "Christ-like." However, to meet face to face with the Christ of the New Testament would come only after one had risen to the higher states of consciousness. This is, of course, conjecture because the question is almost unanswerable even though a grain of truth persists.
4. Do not allow your interest and concern for life after death to blur your responsibilities and attention to the here and now.
5. Marriage as we celebrate it on this side does not exist on the other side.
6. The devil, as portrayed by over-zealous individuals with extremely active imaginations, does not exist, although good and evil are real.
7. Life after death is a fact for all.
8. Persons of all faiths, creeds and races survive physical death and continue their life's journey.
9. Cherished and loved pets survive and are eventually reunited with their masters.
10. The terms "psychic research" and "occult" do not have the same meaning. Telepathy, clairvoyance, clairaudience, precognition, clairsentience and psychokinesis, to name a few, are not to be labeled occult. These facets of psychic phenomena are not demonic, nor do they have anything to do with a mythical devil.
11. A suicide takes his problems with him, is earthbound, in a subjective hell until he repents of his ways and comes to grips with his mental and emotional problems.
12. Develop your own psychic abilities and do not consult sensitives although no great harm will come to those who occasionally seek a sitting with a reputable sensitive.

SOURCE NOTES
1. Hick, John. *The Center of Christianity*. New York: Harper & Row, 1968, p. 114.

SCHEMA FOR WHAT HAPPENS AFTER DEATH

Death is Painless
Death-bed Visions
The Physical Body and the Spiritual
Body Separate
We are Met by Loved Ones
Rest and Recuperation
The Reception Center
Review of Earth Life
Self-Judgment
We Reap What We Sow
We Go to Our Self-Appointed Level
Like Attracts Like

MIND CONTROLS ALL THINGS

THE WHOLE PERSON SURVIVES

FREE WILL PREVAILS

THE PRIMACY OF THOUGHT

WHAT TO EXPECT

Spiritual Body an Exact Replica of
the Physical
Environment Similar to Earth
The World of Spirit is Tangible and
Solid
No Change Geographically
Levels of Consciousness Have
Different Rates of Vibration
All Levels Interpenetrate
No Time or Space as We Know It
Freedom from Earth's Limitations
No Immediate Change in Character

Not All-Knowing on the Other Side
We Revert to the Prime of Life
No Need for Food or Sleep
No Economic Worries

**LIFE IS EVOLUTIONARY
PROGRESSIVE
DEVELOPMENTAL**

EVERYDAY LIFE ON THE OTHER SIDE

Occupations - Schools - Libraries - Museums - Music - Art - Hobbies - All Forms of Recreation - Sports - Art Galleries - Theaters - Clubs and Social Organizations - Cities - Towns - Villages - The Beauties and Wonders of Nature - Permanence and Not Decay

LOVE IS THE HEARTBEAT OF CREATION

A Selected Bibliography

This is an eclectic bibliography, what appears to be best, from many sources. The large selection of books covers not only survival of consciousness but others that have relevance to the topic. I have included many of the classics in the several fields covered. ·They can be read with confidence because they *are* classics.

Some of the volumes mentioned are out of print but, with some exceptions, can be obtained through inter-library loan, or from the libraries of such organizations as Spiritual Frontiers Fellowship, Box 7868, Philadelphia, PA 19101 and the Association for Research and Enlightenment, Virginia Beach, VA. It has been my personal experience that if you want a book badly enough it can be obtained. I also recommend when you are searching for books you look in thrift stores, such as Goodwill and the Salvation Army. I have frequently found many treasures for a pittance.

Some of the books I've listed are not the easiest to read but with effort and perseverance you won't have too much difficulty. They can frequently be the most rewarding. A case in point is Emanuel Swedenborg's *Heaven and Hell.*

Alger, William R. *History of the Doctrine of a Future Life.* Boston: Roberts Brothers, 1889.
Anderson, Bernhard W. *Rediscovering the Bible.* New York: Association Press, 1951.
Angoff, Allan (ed.). *The Psychic Force.* New York: G. P. Putnam's Sons, 1970.
Ashby, Robert. *The Guide Book for Study of the Paranormal.* York Beach, Maine: Samuel Weiser, 1987. Revised Edition.
Augustine, St. *Confessions.* Trans. Edward Bouverie Pusey. Franklin Center, Pennsylvania: The Franklin Library, 1982..
Aurelius, Marcus. *Meditations.* New York: Walter J. Black, 1945.
Baird, A. T. *One Hundred Cases for Survival After Death.* New York: Bernard Ackerman, 1944.
Balfour, G. W. *The Ear of Dionysus.* Proceedings of the Society for Psychical Research. Vol. XXIX, pp. 197-243.
Bander, Peter. *Voices from the Tapes.* New York: Drake Publishers, 1973.

Banks, Hal. *Introduction to Psychic Studies*. Bend, Oregon: Maverick Publications, 1980.
Barbanell, Maurice. *This is Spiritualism*. New York: Award Books, 1967.
Barbanell, Sylvia. *When Your Animal Dies*. London: Psychic Press, 1944.
Barclay, William. *A Spiritual Autobiography*. Grand Rapids, Michigan: William Eerdmans, 1975.
– –. *The Apostles' Creed for Everyman*. New York: Harper & Row, 1967.
Barrett, William. *Death Bed Visions*. London: Methuen & Co., 1926.
Bauman, Edward W. *The Life and Teaching of Jesus*. Philadelphia: The Westminster Press, 1960.
Bayless, Raymond. *The Other Side of Death*. New Hyde Park, New York: University Books, 1971.
Beard, Paul. *Living On*. New York: Continuum Publishing Co., 1981.
– –. *Survival of Death*. London: Psychic Press, 1972.
Becker, Ernest. *The Denial of Death*. New York: Free Press, 1973.
Benson, Herbert. *The Relaxation Response*. New York: William Morrow, 1975.
Biographical Dictionary of Parapsychology. New York: Helix Press, 1964.
Blackmore, Susan J. *Beyond the Body*. London: A Paladin Book, 1983.
Bonnell, John Sutherland. *I Believe in Immortality*. New York: Abingdon Press, 1959.
Borgia, Anthony. *Life in the World Unseen*. London: Psychic Press, 1969.
– –. *More about Life in the World Unseen*. San Francisco: H. G. White, 1968.
– –. *Here and Hereafter*. London: Odhams Press, 1959.
Bozzano, Ernesto. *Discarnate Influence in Human Life*. London: John M. Watkins, no publication date.
Bradley, Dennis. *The Wisdom of the Gods*. London: T. Werner Laurie, 1925.
– –. *Towards the Stars*. London: T. Werner Laurie, no publication date.

Bibliography 141

Broad, C. D. *Religion, Philosophy and Psychical Research.* New York: Humanities Press, 1969.
— —. *Human Identity and Survival.* F. W. H. Myers Memorial Lecture. Society for Psychical Research. London: 1958.
— —. *Lectures on Psychical Research.* New York: The Humanities Press, 1962.
Brown, Slater. *The Heyday of Spiritualism.* New York: Pocket Books, 1972.
Capra, Fritjof. *The Tao of Physics.* New York: Bantam Books, 1977.
Carrington, Hereward. *The Case of Psychic Survival.* New York: Citadel Press, 1957.
Cavendish, Richard (ed.). *Encyclopedia of the Unexplained.* New York: McGraw-Hill, 1974.
Census of Hallucinations. Published in 1894 by the Society for Psychical Research. See: Proceedings, 1894, Part 26. Also see: G. N. M. Tyrrell's Book, *Apparitions,* for an excellent report on the Census.
Cerminara, Gina. *Many Mansions.* New York: William Sloane Associates, 1950.
Cerutti, Edwina. *Olga Worrall: Mystic with the Healing Hands.* NewYork: Harper & Row, 1975.
Choron, Jacques. *Death and Modern Man.* New York: Collier Books, 1964.
Clair St., David. *Watseka.* Chicago: Playboy Press, 1977.
Clarke, William Newton. *An Outline of Christian Theology.* New York: Charles Scribner's Sons. 1898.
Conway, Flo and Siegelman, Jim. *Holy Terror.* Garden City, New York: Doubleday & Co., 1982.
Cranston, Sylvia and Carey Williams. *Reincarnation: A New Horizon in Science, Religion, and Society.* New York: Julian Press, 1984.
Crenshaw, James. *Telephone Between Worlds.* Los Angeles: DeVorss & Co., 1950.
Crookall, Robert. *The Next World – and the Next.* London: The Theosophical Publishing House, 1966.
— —. *Intimations of Immortality.* London: James Clarke & Co., 1965.
— —. *The Supreme Adventure.* London: The Camelot Press, 1961.
Crookes, William. *Phenomena of Spiritualism.* London: J. Burns, 1874.

Cummins, Geraldine. *The Road to Immortality*. London: Ivor Nicholson & Watson, 1933.
– –. *Beyond Human Personality*. London: Psychic Press, 1952.
– –. *Mind in Life and Death*. London: The Aquarian Press, 1956.
– –. *Swan on a Black Sea*. London: Routledge and Kegan Paul, 1965.
Currie, Ian. *You Cannot Die*. New York: Methuen, 1978.
Davis, Andrew Jackson. *The Great Harmonia*. New York: Sanborn Carter & Bazin, 5 vols., 1956.
Dickens, Charles. *The Mystery of Edwin Drood*. New York: Everyman's Library, 1915.
Dodds, E. R. *Why I Do Not Believe in Survival*. Proceedings of the Society for Psychical Research. Vol. XLII: pp. 147-72, 1934.
Doyle, Arthur Conan. *The History of Spiritualism*. 2 vols. London: Cassell and Co., 1926.
– –. *The New Revelation*. London: Hodder and Stoughton, 1918.
Ducasse, C. J. *The Belief in a Life After Death*. Springfield, Illinois: Charles C. Thomas, 1961.
Dusen, Wilson Van. *The Presence of Other Worlds*. New York: Harper & Row, 1974.
Drummond, Henry. *Natural Law in the Spiritual World*. Hodder and Stoughton, 1885.
Dunne, J. W. *An Experiment in Time*. London: Faber and Faber, 1973.
Eagle, White. *Sunrise*. Liss, Hampshire, England: The White Eagle Publishing Trust, 1958.
Ebon, Martin (ed.). *True Experiences in Communicating with the Dead*. New York: Signet, 1959.
– –. *The Evidence for Life After Death*. New York: Signet, 1977.
Eddy, Sherwood. *You Will Survive After Death*. Evanston, Illinois: Clark Publishing Co., 1966.
Elliott, Maurice. *The Psychic Life of Jesus*. London: Spiritualist Press, 1964.
– –. *The Bible as Psychic History*. London: Rider & Co., 1959.
The Encyclopedia of Philosophy. 4 volumes. New York: Macmillan Publishing Co., and the Free Press, 1967.
Feifel, Herman (ed.). *The Meaning of Death*. New York: McGraw-Hill, 1959.
Findlay, Arthur. *On the Edge of the Etheric*. London: The

Psychic Press, 1931.
— —. *Where Two Worlds Meet*. London: The Psychic Press, 1951.
— —. *The Way of Life*. London: The Psychic Press, 1953.
Fodor, Nandor. *An Encyclopaedia of Psychic Science*. Secaucus, New Jersey: The Citadel Press, 1966.
Ford, Arthur. (As told to Jerome Ellison). *The Life Beyond Death*. New York: G. P. Putnam's Sons, 1971.
Forman, Joan. *The Mask of Time*. London: Corgi Books, 1981.
Fortune, Dion. *Through the Gates of Death*. London: The Aquarian Press, 1972.
Fox, Emmet. *Power Through Constructive Thinking*. New York: Harper & Brothers, 1940.
Fuller, John G. *The Ghost of 29 Megacycles*. New York: Signet, 1986.
— —. *The Airmen Who Would Not Die*. New York: G. P. Putnam's Sons, 1979.
Garrett, Eileen J. *Many Voices*. New York: G. P. Putnam's Sons, 1968.
— —. (ed.). *Does Man Survive Death*. New York: Helix Press, 1957.
Gauld, Alan. *Mediumship and Survival*. London: Paladin Books, 1983.
Goldsmith, Joel. *The Art of Meditation*. New York: Harper & Row, 1956.
Gordon, David C. *Overcoming the Fear of Death*. New York: Macmillan Co., 1970.
Great Books of the Western World. 54 Vols. Vols. II & III (A Syntopicon). *The Great Ideas*. Chicago: Encyclopaedia Britannica, 1952. A treasure house of knowledge. Check Syntopicon for topics: Immortality, Life and Death, Man, Mind, Punishment, Soul.
Greaves, Helen. *The Testimony of Light*. London: The Churches' Fellowship for Psychical and Spiritual Studies, 1975.
— —. *The Challenging Light*. Suffolk, England: Neville Spearman, 1984.
Greber, Johannes. *Communication with the Spirit World*. Teaneck, New Jersey: Johannes Greber Memorial Foundation, 1932.
Greeley, Andrew M. *Confessions of a Parish Priest*. New York: Pocket Books, 1987.
Greenhouse, Herbert B., *The Astral Journey*. New York: Doubleday & Co., 1975.

Gurney, Edmund, Myers, F. W. H. and Podmore, Frank. *Phantasms of the Living.* 1 Vol. Abridged. New Hyde Park, New York: University Books, 1962.
Hampton, Charles. *The Transition Called Death.* Wheaton, Illinois: Theosophical Publishing House, 1979.
A Handbook of Christian Theology (ed.). New York: The World Publishing Co., 1958.
Harlow, Ralph. *A Life After Death.* Garden City, New York: Doubleday & Co., 1961.
Hart, Hornell. *The Enigma of Survival.* London: Rider & Co., 1959.
Heaney, John J. *The Sacred & the Psychic.* New York: Paulist Press, 1984.
Hick, John. *Death & Eternal Life.* London: Collins, 1976.
– –. *The Center of Christianity.* NY: Harper & Row, 1968.
Higgins-Pearce, J.D. and Whitby, G. Stanley. *Life, Death & Psychical Research.* London: Rider and Co., 1973.
Hill, J. Arthur. *Spiritualism.* New York: George H. Doran Co., 1919.
Holzer, Hans. *Life After Death.* New York: A Dell Book, 1969.
– –. *Beyond This Life.* Los Angeles: Pinnacle Books, 1969.
Irion, Paul E. *The Funeral: Vestige or Value?* Nashville: Parthenon Press, 1966.
Jacobson, Nils O. *Life Without Death.* New York: Dell Publishing Co., 1971.
James, William. *Principles of Psychology.* 1 Vol. Abridgment. New York: Fawcett Publications, 1963.
– –. *Varieties of Religious Experience.* New York: The Modern Library, 1902.
Johnson, Raynor. *The Imprisoned Splendour.* New York: Harper & Row, 1953.
– –. *Nurslings of Immortality.* New York: Harper & Brothers, 1957.
– –. *A Religious Outlook for Modern Man.* London: Hodder and Stoughton, 1963.
– –. *Psychical Research.* New York: Funk and Wagnalls, 1955.
Jones, E. Stanley. *Is the Kingdom of God Realism?* New York: Abingdon-Cokesbury Press, 1940.
Jung, C.G. *Memories, Dreams, Reflections.* New York: Vintage Books, 1961.
Keller, Helen. *My Religion.* New York: Swedenborg Foundation,

1972.
Kelsey, Morton. *Afterlife*. New York: Paulist Press, 1979.
Klimo, Jon. *Channeling*. Los Angeles: Jeremy P. Tarcher, Inc., 1987.
Knight, David C. (ed.). *The ESP Reader*. New York: Grosset & Dunlap, 1969.
Koestenbaum, Peter. *Is There an Answer to Death?* Englewood Cliffs, New Jersey: Prentice-Hall, 1976.
Koestler, Arthur. *The Roots of Coincidence*. New York: Random House, 1972.
Kubler-Ross, Elisabeth. *On Death and Dying*. New York: Macmillan Co., 1969.
— —. *Questions and Answers on Death and Dying*. New York: Macmillan Co., 1974.
— —. *Death: The Final Stage of Growth*. Englewood Cliffs, New Jersey: Prentice-Hall, 1975.
Kurtz, Paul (ed.). *A Skeptic's Handbook of Parapsychology*. New York: Prometheus Books, 1985.
Lamont, Corliss. *The Illusion of Immortality*. New York: Philosophical Library, 1959.
Langley, Noel. *Edgar Cayce on Reincarnation*. New York: Paperback Library, 1967.
Leadbeater, C. W. *The Other Side of Death*. London: Theosophical Publishing Society, 1904.
Leonard, Gladys Osborne. *My Life in Two Worlds*. London: Cassell & Co., 1931.
Leonard, John C. *The Higher Spiritualism*. Washington, D. C.: The Philosophic Book Co., 1927.
Lester, Reginald M. *In Search of the Hereafter*. New York: Wilfred Funk, 1953.
Lodge, Oliver. *The Survival of Man*. London: Methuen & Co., 1909.
— —. *Past Years*. New York: Charles Scribner's Sons, 1932.
Lombroso, Cesare. *After Death-What?* Boston: Small, Maynard & Co., 1909.
Lorimer, David. *Survival?* London: Routledge & Kegan Paul, 1984.
MacGregor, Geddes. *Reincarnation in Christianity*. Wheaton, Illinois: The Theosophical Publishing House, 1978.
Mackenzie, Andrew. *Hauntings and Apparitions*. London: Paladin, 1983.

Marchant, James. (ed.). *Survival*. New York: G. P.. Putnam's Sons, 1924.
Marlow, Christopher. *Tragical History of Dr. Faustus*. New York: Appleton-Century-Crofts. 1950.
Marryat, Florence. *There is No Death*. New York: Causeway Books, 1973.
Matson, Archie. *Afterlife*. New York: Harper & Row, 1975.
Meek, George W. *After We Die, What Then?* Franklin, North Carolina: Metascience Corporation, 1980.
Milton, John. *Paradise Lost*. New York: Odyssey Press, 1962.
Mitchell, Edgar (ed.). *Psychic Exploration*. New York: G. P. Putnam's Sons, 1974.
Montgomery, Ruth. *Here and Hereafter*. New York: Fawcett, 1969.
– –. *A World Beyond*. New York: Coward, McCann & Geoghegan, 1971.
– –. *Herald of the New Age*. New York: Fawcett Crest, 1986.
Moody, Raymond A., Jr. *Life After Life*. Carmel, New York: Guideposts, 1975.
Moore, R. Laurence. *In Search of White Crows*. New York: Oxford University Press, 1977.
Moses, Stainton. *Spirit Teachings*. London: Spiritualist Press, 1962.
Muhl, Anita M. *Automatic Writing*. New York: Helix Press, 1963.
Muldoon, Sylvan, Hereward Carrington. *The Projection of the Astral Body*. New York: Samuel Weiser, Inc., 1970.
Mundy, Jon. *Learning to Die*. Evanston, Illinois: Spiritual Frontiers Fellowship, 1973.
Murphy, Gardner. *Three Papers on the Survival Problem*. New York: The American Society for Psychical Research, 1945.
– –. *William James on Psychical Research*. New York: The Viking Press, 1960.
– –. *Challenge of Psychical Research*. New York: Harper & Brothers, 1961.
Myers, F. W. H. *Human Personality and Its Survival of Bodily Death*. 2 Vols. New Hyde Park, New York: University Books, 1961.
Neff, H. R. *Psychic Phenomena and Religion*. Philadelphia: Westminster Press, 1971.

Osis, Karlis. *Deathbed Observations of Physicians and Nurses.* New York: Parapsychology Foundation, 1961.
– –. and Erlendur Haraldsson. *At the Hour of Death.* New York: Avon Books, 1977.
Parrott, Wanda Sue. *Automatic Writing.* Los Angeles: Sherbourne Press, 1974.
Perry, Michael. *Psychic Studies: A Christian's View.* Wellingborough, Northamptonshire, England: The Aquarian Press, 1984.
Peters, Madison C. *After Death What?* New York: The Christian Herald Bible House, 1908.
Pike, James A. *If This Be Heresy.* New York: Harper and Row, 1967.
– –. *The Other Side.* New York: Doubleday & Co., 1968.
Piper, Alta. *The Life and Work of Mrs. Piper.* London: Kegan Paul, Trench, Trubner & Co., 1929.
Podmore, Frank. *Mediums of the 19th Century.* 2 Vols. New Hyde Park, New York: University Books, 1963.
Pole, Wellesley Tudor. *Private Dowding.* Cattedown, Plymouth, England: Neville Spearman, 1966.
Powel, T. Rowland. *The Psychic Message of the Scriptures.* Reigate, Surrey, England: The Omega Press, 1954.
Prince, Walter Franklin. *The Case of Patience Worth.* New Hyde Park, New York: University Books, 1964.
Proceedings and Journals. Society for Psychical Research, London: Primary Documents dating from 1882.
Proceedings and Journals. American Society for Psychical Research, New York: Primary documents dating from 1907.
Randall, J. *Parapsychology and the Nature of Life.* New York: Harper & Row, 1975.
Randall, Neville. *Life After Death.* London: Robert Hale & Co., 1974.
Report on Occult and Psychic Activities. New York: Office of the General Assembly, United Presbyterian Church in the U. S. A., 1976.
Rhine, J. B. and Pratt, J. G. *Parapsychology.* Rev. Ed., Springfield, Illinois: Thomas, 1974.
Rhine, L. E. *Psi, What is It?* New York: Harper & Row, 1976.
Richmond, Kenneth. *Evidence of Identity.* London: G. Bell and Sons, 1939.
Richmond, Zoe. *Evidence of Purpose.* London: G. Bell and Sons,

1938.
Riland, George. *The New Steinerbooks Dictionary of the Paranormal*. New York: Warner Books, 1980.
Ring, Kenneth. *Life at Death*. New York: Coward, McCann & Geoghegan, 1980.
— —. *Heading Toward Omega*. New York: William Morrow, 1984.
Rogo, D. Scott and Raymond Bayless. *Phone Calls from the Dead*. New York: Berkley Book, 1979.
— —. *The Welcoming Silence*. Secaucus, New Jersey: University Books, 1973.
— —. *Life After Death*. Wellingborough, Northamptonshire, England: The Aquarian Press, 1986.
Rokeach, Milton. *The Open and Closed Mind*. New York: Basic Books, 1960.
Salter, W. H. *Zoar: The Evidence of Psychical Research Concerning Survival*. London: Sidgwick and Jackson, 1961.
Sanford, Agnes. *The Healing Light*. St. Paul, Minnesota: Macalester Park Publishing Co., 1972.
Sherman, Harold. *You Live After Death*. Greenwich, Connecticut: Fawcett Publications, 1972.
— —. *You Can Communicate with the Unseen World*. Greenwich, Connecticut: Fawcett Publications, 1974.
— —. *The Dead are Alive*. Amherst, Wisconsin: Amherst Press, 1981.
Sinclair, Upton. *Mental Radio*. New York: Collier Books, 1971.
Smith, Alson J. *Immortality: The Scientific Evidence*. New York: New American Library, 1967.
Smith, Leslie R. *From Sunset to Dawn*. Nashville: Abingdon Press, 1979.
Smith, Susy. *The Mediumship of Mrs. Leonard*. New Hyde Park, New York: University Books, 1964.
— —. *Do We Live after Death*. New York: Manor Books, 1974.
— —. *Life is Forever*. New York: G. P. Putnam's Sons, 2975.
— —. *The Book of James*. New York: G. P. Putnam's Sons, 1974.
Spence, Lewis. *An Encyclopaedia of Occultism*. New York: New American Library, 1974.
Stead, W. T. *After Death*. London: Psychic Book Club, 1952.
Steiger, Brad. *The World Beyond Death*. Norfolk, Virginia: The Donning Co., 1982.
Stevenson, Ian. *Twenty Cases Suggestive of Reincarnation*. New

York: American Society for Psychical Research, 1966.
Stevens, William O. *Beyond the Sunset.* New York: Dodd, Mead & Co., 1945.
Stobart, St. Clair. *Ancient Lights.* London: Kegan Paul, Trench, Trubner and Co., 1923.
Stowe, Harriet Beecher. *Uncle Tom's Cabin.* New York: Modern Library, 1938.
Streeter, H. Burnett, Brock-Clutton A., Emmet, C. W., and Hadfield, J.A. *Immortality.* London: Macmillan and Co., 1917.
Swedenborg, Emanuel. *The Divine Providence.* New York: The Swedenborg Foundation, 1970.
– –. *Heaven and Hell.* New York: Swedenborg Foundation, 1971.
Synnestvedt, Sig. *The Essential Swedenborg.* New York: Swedenborg Foundation, 1981.
Thomas, Charles Drayton. *Some New Evidence for Human Survival.* London: W. Collins Sons & Co., 1922.
– –. *Life Beyond Death with Evidence.* London: W. Collins Sons & Co., 1937.
Thomas, Lewis. *The Lives of a Cell.* New York: Viking Press, 1974.
Toynbee, Arnold and Koestler, Arthur (and others). *Life After Death.* New York: McGraw-Hill Book Co., 1976.
Tweedale, Charles L. *Man's Survival After Death.* London: Grant Richards, 1925.
–-. *News from the Next World.* London: Spiritualist Press, 1947.
Tyrrell, G. N. M. *The Personality of Man.* Baltimore: Penguin Books, 1947.
– –. *Apparitions.* New York: Collier Books, 1963.
Walker, Nea. *The Bridge: A Case for Survival.* London: Cassell, 1927.
Weatherhead, Leslie D. *After Death.* New York: Abingdon Press, (no publication date).
– –. *The Christian Agnostic.* New York: Abingdon Press, 1965.
– –. *Life Begins at Death.* Nashville: Abingdon Press, 1969.
White, John. *A Practical Guide to Death and Dying.* Wheaton, Illinois: Theosophical Publishing House, 1980.
White, R. A. and Dale, L. A. *Parapsychology: Sources of Information.* Metuchen, New Jersey: Scarecrow Press, 1973.
White, Stewart Edward. *The Betty Book.* New York: E. P. Dutton and Co., 1937.

— —. *The Unobstructed Universe*. New York: E. P. Dutton and Co., 1941.
Wickland, Carl A. *30 Years Among the Dead*. Hollywood: Newcastle Publishing Co., 1974.
Wilson, James Bright. *Pathetic Protestant Preachers*. Claremont, California: Prudence Press, 1985.
Woodman, Pardoe and Stead, Estelle. *Blue Island*. London: Hutchinson & Co., 1922.
Wolman, Benjmin B. (ed.). *Handbook of Parapsychology*. New York: Van Nostrand Reinhold Co., 1977.
Worth, Patience. *Light from Beyond*. (Dictated through Mrs. John H. Curran.) Selected by Herman Behr. New York: Patience Worth Publishing Co., 1923.
— —. *The Pot Upon the Wheel*. (Dictated through Mrs. John H. Curran.) St. Louis: The Dorset Press, 1921.

Books For The Inquiring Mind

Abingdon Dictionary of Living Religions. Gen. Ed. Keith Crim. Nashville: Abingdon, 1981.
Barclay, William. *The Daily Study Bible Series*. 18 Vols. New Testament. Revised Edition. Philadelphia: Westminster Press.
— —. *Introducing the Bible*. London: The Bible Reading Fellowship, 1972.
Blair, Edward P. *Abingdon Bible Handbook*. Nashville: Abingdon Press, 1975.
Brown, Robert McAfee. *The Bible Speaks to You*. Philadelphia: Westminster Press, 1955.
Cerminara, Gina. *Insights for the Age of Aquarius*. Englewood Cliffs, New Jersey: Prentice-Hall, 1973.
Foote, Henry Wilder. *The Religion of an Inquiring Mind*. Boston: The Beacon Press, 1955.
Hick, John. *The Center of Christianity*. New York: Harper & Row, 1968.
The Interpreter's Dictionary of the Bible. Ed. George A. Buttrick. 4 Vols. Nashville: Abingdon Press, 1962.
Jones, Stanley. *Is the Kingdom of God Realism?* Nashville: Abingdon Cokesbury Press, 1940.
Kung, Hans. *The Church*. New York: Sheed and Ward, 1967.
— —. *On Being a Christian*. Garden City, New York: Doubleday

& Co., 1976.
– –. *Eternal Life*. Garden City, New York: Doubleday & Co., 1984.
Laymon, Charles M. (ed.). *The Interpreter's One-Volume Commentary on the Bible*. Nashville: Abingdon Press, 1971.
Neil, William. *Harper's Bible Commentary*. New York: Harper & Row, 1962.
The New International Dictionary of the Christian Church. Gen. Ed. J. D. Douglas. Revised. Grand Rapids, Michigan: Zondervon, 1974.
Phillips, J. B. *Ring of Truth*. New York: Macmillan Co., 1967.
Smith, Huston. *The Religions of Man*. New York: Perennial Library, 1958.
Trueblood, Elton D. *Philosophy of Religion*. New York: Harper & Brothers, 1957.
Wells, Donald A. *God, Man and the Thinker*. New York: Random House, 1962.

Books to Help Nourish Your Spiritual Life

Bach, Marcus. *The Will to Believe*. Englewood Cliffs, New Jersey: Prentice-Hall, 1955.
Baillie, John. *A Diary of Private Prayer*. Nashville: Abingdon Press, 1975.
Buttrick, George A. *Prayer*. Nashville: Abingdon-Cokesbury Press, 1942.
Campbell, Donald J. *The Adventure of Prayer*. Nashville: Abingdon-Cokesbury, 1949.
Drummond, Henry. *The Greatest Thing in the World*. London: Collins, (no publication date).
Ferre, Nels. *Strengthening the Spiritual Life*. New York: Harper & Brothers, 1947.
Fosdick, Harry Emerson. *The Meaning of Prayer*. New York: Association Press, 1942.
Harkness, Georgia. *Prayer and the Common Life*. New York: Abingdon-Cokesbury, 1948.
Kelly, Thomas R. *A Testament of Devotion*. New York: Harper & Brothers, 1941.
Kempis, Thomas a. *The Imitation of Christ*. London: Collins,

1960.
Lawrence, Brother. *The Practice of the Presence of God.* Old Tappan, New Jersey: Fleming H. Revell, 1974.
LeShan, Lawrence. *How to Meditate.* New York: Bantam Books, 1974.
Merton, Thomas. *New Seeds of Contemplation.* New York: New Directions Publishing Corporation, 1972.
— —. *The Seven Story Mountain.* New York: Harcourt Brace Jovanovich, 1978.
Nouwen, Henri J. M. *The Way of the Heart.* New York: Ballantine Books, 1981.
— —. *Reaching Out.* Garden City, New York: Image Books, 1986.
Parker, William and St. Johns, Elaine. *Prayer Can Change Your Life.* Englewood Cliffs, New Jersey: Prentice-Hall, 1957.
Sampson, Tom. *Cultivating the Presence.* New York: Thomas Y. Crowell Co., 1977.
Steere, Douglas. *On Beginning from Within.* New York: Harper & Brothers, 1943.
Thurman, Howard. *The Inward Journey.* New York: Harper & Brothers, 1961.

Recommended Translations of The Bible

Revised Standard Version with Apocrypha.
The New English Bible with Apocrypha.
Good News Bible (Today's English Version) with Apocrypha.
The Jerusalem Bible.
New International Version.
New American Standard Bible.

CPSIA information can be obtained
at www.ICGtesting.com
Printed in the USA
LVHW090140290619
622762LV00001B/6/P